Casting Call

By: Anthony Peters

Copyright © by Anthony Peters

This Book is Dedicated to:

My Father and Mother

About this Book:

I was introduced at a young age to some great films by my parents. I was also given a great deal of background on the stars of those films. It seemed that from the start of the motion picture industry there were two viewpoints. One is that the movies gave the stars their success, the other is that the stars made the movies a success. Film fans usually fall into one of these schools of thought. The amount of coverage given to stars would indicate that, in most cases, the latter of the two is more prevalent. Usually I find myself drawn to a film by who is in it.

Are you as a fan able to consider that other actors or actresses were supposed to play the roles that have already been made famous? Well this book will allow you to consider just that. A star of a film who you thought was made for that role was not always the first choice of the casting call. Take a look at what almost was in some of the best films of all time. The choices may reaffirm what you already like, however it is possible you will have a new perspective, one which you prefer. I hope you enjoy reading this book as much as I did writing it.

48 Hours (1982)

- Mickey Rourke turned down the lead role of Detective Jack Cates.

- The role of Jack Cates was played by Nick Nolte.

- Denzel Washington and Richard Pryor were both considered for the role of Reggie Hammond.

- The role of Reggie Hammond was played by Eddie Murphy.

- Kris Kristofferson was also considered for the role of Jack Cates.

- Jeff Bridges turned down the role of Jack Cates because he did not want to do a cop movie.

- Clint Eastwood turned down the role of Jack Cates. He wanted to play the role of Reggie Hammond.

My Take: You can never go wrong with Clint Eastwood. Eddie Murphy was clearly the best choice for his role.

A Beautiful Mind (2001)

- Robert Redford was set to direct the film but pulled out.

- Ron Howard directed the film and won the Academy Award for Best Director.

- Tom Cruise at one time was considered for the lead role of John Nash.

- Russell Crowe played John Nash.

- Salma Hayek was considered for the female lead role of Alicia Larde Nash.

- Jennifer Connelly played Alicia Larde Nash and went on to win the Academy Award for Best Supporting Actress.

- The film won the Academy Award for Best Picture.

My Take: Russell Crowe was not only at the top of his craft, he received an Academy Award Best Actor nomination for the third year in a row.

A Man for All Seasons (1966)

- Richard Harris was considered for the role of King Henry VIII, which was eventually played by Robert Shaw.

- Vanessa Redgrave was the first choice for the role of Margaret but had to drop out due to a conflict in her schedule. The role was then played by Susannah York.

- Fred Zinnemann directed and won the Academy Award for Best Director.

- Won the Academy Award for Best Picture and Screenplay.

- Paul Scofield played Thomas More and won the Academy Award for Best Actor.

- Richard Burton turned down the role of Thomas More.

- The producers wanted Laurence Olivier to play Thomas More and Alec Guiness to play Cardinal Wolsey.

- Director Fred Zinnemann insisted that Paul Scofield play Thomas More and Orson Welles play Cardinal Wolsey, which he did.

- Charlton Heston wanted the lead but was not given serious consideration.

- John Huston turned down the role of the Duke of Norfolk which was played by Nigel Davenport.

My Take: One of the least seen and appreciated Academy Award winning Best Pictures.

A Streetcar Named Desire (1951)

- Olivia de Havilland turned down the role of Blanche DuBois.

Casting Call

- Jessica Tandy at one time was set to play Blanche DuBois.

- The role of Blanche was then given to Vivian Leigh to have more box office appeal. She won the Academy Award for Best Actress.

- Karl Malden played the role of Mitch and won the Academy Award for Best Supporting Actor.

- Kim Hunter played Stella Kowalski and won the Academy Award for Best Supporting Actress.

- John Garfield turned down the role Stanley Kowalski.

- Marlon Brando played Stanley Kowalski and received an Oscar nomination for Best Actor.

My Take: Brando should have won the Academy Award for Best Actor in one of his most famous performances.

The African Queen (1951)

- John Mills and Bette Davis were the top choice for the male and female lead roles.

- Bette Davis was offered the role in 1938 with David Niven to play Charlie.

- In 1947 Bette Davis was again offered the lead female role, this time with James Mason as Charlie. She had to decline because of her pregnancy.

- In 1949 when Bette Davis tried out for the lead female role again the direction was already set to have Katherine Hepburn star.

- Humphrey Bogart starred as Charlie Allnut and won the Academy Award for Best Actor.

- Katherine Hepburn did play the role of Rose Sayer.

- Paul Henreid and Charles Laughton at one time were also considered for the role of Charlie Allnut.

- Columbia studios originally bought the movie to star Charles Laughton and his wife Elsa Lanchester. In 1938 they filmed The Beachcomber which was the same story but not a success at the box office.

- The African Queen was directed by John Huston.

Air Force One (1997)

- Kevin Costner turned down the lead role of President James Marshall because he was filming The Postman (1997) at the time. Costner then suggested Harrison Ford for the role.

- Harrison Ford played President James Marshall.

- Arnold Schwarzenegger, Keanu Reeves and Dennis Quaid were all considered for the lead role if Harrison Ford turned it down.

My Take: Given his well known political ambitions, Arnold would have been a great choice to play the president.

An Affair to Remember (1957)

- Ingrid Bergman was the first choice to play the female lead of Terry McKay.

- Doris Day was also considered for the role of Terry McKay.

- Deborah Kerr played the role of Terry McKay.

- Cary Grant played the male lead role of Nickie Ferrante.

Animal House (1978)

- Bill Murray, Chevy Chase, Dan Aykroyd, and Brian Doyle-Murray all turned down roles in the film because of prior commitments.

- Director John Landis wanted Bill Murray to play Eric "Otter" Stratton and Chevy Chase to play Donald "Boone" Schoenstein. Those roles were eventually played by Tim Matheson and Peter Riegert respectively.

- The role of Daniel Simpson Day or "D-Day" was written for Dan Aykroyd. The role was played in the film by Bruce McGill.

- Rock n Roll singer Meatloaf was the second choice to star as John "Bluto" Blutarsky, who was played by John Belushi.

- Jack Webb was the first choice to play Dean Vernon Wormer; eventually the part was played by John Vernon.

- Kim Novak was the first choice to play Mrs. Marion Wormer, played by Verna Bloom in the film.

- Harold Ramis, of Ghostbusters fame, wrote the role of Boone with himself in mind to star.

- John Landis thought Harold Ramis was too old, even though Ramis was 32 years old and Peter Riegert, who played Boone was already 29 years old himself.

My Take: Bill Murray and Dan Aykroyd would have fit right in. Murray is a comic legend with one of the best deliveries ever.

Apocalypse Now (1979)

- Nick Nolte wanted to play the role of Captain Benjamin L. Willard.

- Jeff Bridges auditioned to play Captain Willard.

- Harvey Keitel was cast as Captain Benjamin L. Willard; however Director Francis Ford Coppolla replaced him with Martin Sheen.

- Director Francis Ford Coppolla asked Jack Nicholson and Al Pacino to play Captain Willard but they both turned the role down.

- Marlon Brando starred as Colonel Walter E. Kurtz.

- Other then Marlon Brando, director Francis Ford Coppolla considered Jack Nicholson, Robert Redford and Al Pacino for the role of Colonel Walter E. Kurtz.

- Coppolla's first choice for Colonel Lucas was James Caan but his asking price was too high.

- Harrison Ford played the role of Colonel Lucas.

My Take: One of many roles James Caan should have just accepted. You can never go wrong with Brando.

Arsenic and Old Lace (1944)

- Ronald Reagan and Jack Benny were each offered the role of Mortimer Brewster but both turned it down.

- Cary Grant played Mortimer Brewster.

- Bob Hope was offered the lead role of Mortimer Brewster and accepted, however Paramount Studios would not allow him to act in a Warner Bros. film because he was under contract to them.

- Frank Capra directed the film.

My Take: Bob Hope would have been very good in this role as well but Cary Grant certainly nailed it.

Assassins (1995)

- Sylvester Stallone played Robert Rath. Michael Douglas and Arnold Schwarzenegger were considered for Robert Rath.

- Christian Slater turned down the role of Miguel Bain.

- Woody Harrelson and Tom Cruise were both considered for the role of Miguel Bain.

- Antonio Banderas played Miguel Bain.

- Mel Gibson was set to direct but decided not to and instead passed it along to his friend Richard Donner, who directed Mel in the Lethal Weapon films.

My Take: Stallone is never the wrong choice for a thriller or action movie. He was the best choice for this film.

Back to the Future (1985)

- Michael J. Fox played Marty McFly.

- Eric Stoltz was cast as Marty because Michael J. Fox had a scheduling problem that was eventually worked out so Fox could play the role.

- C. Thomas Howell and singer Corey Hart were both considered for the role of Marty.

- Christopher Lloyd played Doc Brown.

- John Lithgow and Jeff Goldblum were under consideration for the role of Doc Brown.

- Ralph Macchio (of Karate Kid fame) declined the role of Marty McFly.

My Take: Eric Stoltz and Ralph Macchio would really like to have this opportunity back.

Batman (1989)

- Michael Keaton played the title role of Bruce Wayne/ Batman.

- Also considered at one time for the role of Batman: Jeff Bridges, Emilio Estevez, Kevin Costner, Matthew Broderick, Tom Cruise, Harrison Ford, Robert Downey Jr., Kevin Spacey, Dennis Quaid, Kurt Russell, Arnold Schwarzenegger, Charlie Sheen, Bill Murray, Pierce Brosnan, Tom Selleck, Daniel Day Lewis and Bruce Willis.

- Kim Basinger played the female lead role of Vicki Vale.

- Sean Young was cast as Vicki Vale; however she suffered an injury and had to drop out.

- Under consideration for the female lead role of Vicki Vale: Jamie Lee Curtis, Ellen Barkin, Kate Capshaw, Glenn Close, Madonna, Geena Davis, Mia Farrow, Carrie Fisher, Bridget Fonda, Jodie Foster, Teri Garr, Melanie Griffith, Daryl Hannah, Linda Hamilton, Barbara Hershey, Amy Irving, Kay Lenz, Diane Lane, Jessica Lange, Lori Loughlin, Kelly McGillis, Catherine O'Hara, Tatum O'Neal, Molly Ringwald, Jane Seymour, Brooke Shields, Cybill Shepherd, Sissy Spacek, Sharon Stone, Lea Thompson, Deborah Winger and Sela Ward.

- Jack Nicholson played the role of Jack Napier/The Joker.

- The following actors were considered for the role of The Joker: Robin Williams, Willem Dafoe, David Bowie, John Lithgow, Tim Curry and James Woods.

My Take: I would have taken Tom Selleck or Bruce Willis in the lead and Kay Lenz as Vicki, although Kim Basinger was good.

Batman Begins (2005)

- Actors who auditioned for the role of Bruce Wayne/Batman: Christian Bale, Joshua Jackson, Hugh Dancy, Billy Crudup, Cillian Murphy, Henry Cavill and Jake Gyllenhaal.

- Under consideration for the role of Bruce Wayne/Batman: David Boreanaz and Ashton Kutcher.

- Christian Bale played Bruce Wayne/Batman.

- Chris Cooper declined the role of Jim Gordon.

- Kurt Russell and Dennis Quaid were both considered for the role of Jim Gordon.

- Gary Oldman played Jim Gordon.

- Viggo Mortenson turned down the role of Henri Ducard.

- Liam Neeson played Henri Ducard.

- Daniel Day Lewis was approached about playing Henri Ducard.

- Anthony Hopkins was offered the role of Alfred but turned it down.

- Michael Caine played Alfred.

- Laurence Fishburne was considered to play the role of Lucius Fox.

- Morgan Freeman played Lucius Fox.

- Claire Danes and Reese Witherspoon were both considered for the female lead role of Rachel Dawes.

- Katie Holmes eventually played Rachel Dawes.

Ben- Hur (1959)

- Paul Newman declined the lead role of Judah Ben-Hur.

- Burt Lancaster, who was an atheist, claimed he turned down the lead for many reasons, one being that he did not want to promote Christianity.

- Robert Ryan and Stewart Granger were both considered for the role of Messala, which went to Stephen Boyd.

- Charlton Heston played the lead role of Judah Ben-Hur.Charlton Heston won the Academy Award for Best Actor.

- Cesare Danova screen tested for the lead role of Judah Ben-Hur.

- William Wyler directed and won the Academy Award for Best Director.

- Ben Hur won the Academy Award for Best Picture.

- The film won a record eleven Academy Awards.

My Take: When you set the record for most Academy Awards it is hard to argue the choices that were made. This is a great film that lives up to the awards it received.

Beverly Hills Cop (1984)

- Eddie Murphy played the lead role of Axel Foley, taking the role after dropping out of the film Ghostbusters.

- The role of Axel Foley was written for Sylvester Stallone, he then left the movie and went on to use some of the ideas he had for Beverly Hills Cop in the film Cobra (1986).

- Al Pacino, Mickey Rourke and James Caan were considered for the role of Axel Foley.

- Martin Brest directed.

My Take: Clearly with Stallone in the lead this film would have had a different tone and more of a hard edge. That formula is Stallone's bread and butter. The film was released with a comedy first theme and I can't think of anyone who would have played this role better then Eddie Murphy did.

The Blade Runner (1982)

- Harrison Ford played the role of Rick Deckard.

- Dustin Hoffman was the first choice to play Rick.

- Also considered to play Rick Deckard were Tommy Lee Jones, Gene Hackman, Sean Connery, Jack Nicholson, Paul Newman, Clint Eastwood, Arnold Schwarzenegger, Al Pacino, Burt Reynolds, William Devane, Scott Glenn, Robert Duvall, Nick Nolte and Peter Falk.

- Daryl Hannah played the role of Pris.

- Deborah Harry was under consideration for the role of Pris.

- Sean Young played the role of Rachael.

- Victoria Principal and Barbara Hershey were both considered for the role of Rachael.

- Joe Turkel played the role of Tyrell.

- Robert Mitchum and Sterling Hayden were at one time considered for the role of Tyrell.

My Take: Burt Reynolds is totally underrated as an actor and would have been great in the lead. Victoria Principal should have been in more films, this being one of them.

Bourne Identity (2002)

- Brad Pitt turned down the led role of Jason Bourne, played by Matt Damon, to film Spy Game (2001).

My Take: Out of these two choices Brad Pitt would have been far better. Even though he is still one of the top stars this would have taken Pitt's career up even another level.

The Breakfast Club (1985)

- Emilio Estevez was set to play the role of John Bender instead of the role of Andrew Clark, which he ended up playing in the film.

- Molly Ringwald really wanted the role of Allison Reynolds, but the role was promised to Ally Sheedy.

- Ally Sheedy played Allison Reynolds in the film.

- Rick Moranis was cast in the role of the janitor Carl but eventually was replaced by John Kapelos due to creative differences.

- Jodie Foster was considered to play the role of Claire Standish, which was played in the film by Molly Ringwald.

- Brooke Shields was also considered for the role of Allison Reynolds.

- John Cusack was actually cast as John Bender however Director John Hughes replaced him with Judd Nelson.

- Nicholas Cage was the original choice for the role of John Bender but his desired salary was an issue.

- Bryan Ferry, Billy Idol and Chrissie Hynde all turned down the offer to record the theme song 'Don't you forget about me'. Chrissie Hynde then suggested the band Simple Minds because she was married to the lead singer Jim Kerr at that time.

- Simple Minds recorded the song which became a huge number one hit for the group.

My Take: Nicholas Cage would have been great as Bender. This film did find the right feel and the cast was the main reason.

The Bridge on the River Kwai (1957)

- Cary Grant was considered to play the role of Shears after Humphrey Bogart became unavailable. The producer, Sam Spiegel, had his doubts about Grant, so Cary Grant turned the role down.

- Ronald Coleman, Noel Coward, Ray Milland and James Mason were all considered for the role of Shears.

- Laurence Olivier was offered the opportunity to play the role of Shears but turned it down.

- William Holden ended up playing the role of Shears.

- Acclaimed director Howard Hawks was asked to direct the film but declined.

- John Ford and Fred Zinnemann were also considered to direct.

- David Lean then directed the film and won the Academy Award for Best Director.

- John Gielgud was the top choice to play Major Warden.

- Jack Hawkins played the role of Major Warden.

- Charles Laughton and James Mason were at one time approached to play the role of Colonel Nicholson.

- Alec Guiness, who was always the first choice for the role of Colonel Nicholson, played Colonel Nicholson.

- Alec Guiness won the Academy Award for Best Actor.

- Modern film fans know Alec Guiness as Ben Obi-Wan Kenobi in Star Wars (1977).

- The Bridge on the River Kwai won the Academy Award for Best Picture.

My Take: This makes one think like many other films, were the Academy Awards waiting to be won or are the casting and director choices the reason for the Awards? That is for you to decide.

Broken Arrow (1996)

- John Travolta was offered either of the lead roles, which were Major Vic Deakins or Capt. Riley Hale. Travolta chose the role of Major Vic Deakins.
- Christian Slater played the role of Riley Hale.
- Jennifer Aniston was under consideration for the role of Terry Carmichael.
- Samantha Mathis played the role of Terry Carmichael.

Butch Cassidy and the Sundance Kid (1969)

- Marlon Brando was considered for one of the lead roles with Paul Newman taking the other lead.
- Dustin Hoffman was once considered for the role of Butch Cassidy.

- Paul Newman played Butch Cassidy.

- Jack Lemmon and Warren Beatty both said no to the role of the Sundance Kid.

- Robert Redford played the Sundance Kid.

My Take: Brando and Newman would have been great as well. Warren Beatty probably wishes he would have accepted.

Caddyshack (1980)

- The Noonan family was modeled after the family of brothers Bill and Brian Doyle Murray according to director Harold Ramis. There were six Murray brothers in real life.

- Harold Ramis said the part of Ty Webb, which was played by Chevy Chase, was kind of written with Chevy Chase in mind.

- Harold Ramis said they were leaning toward having Mickey Rourke play the role of Danny Noonan, which was eventually played by Michael O'Keefe.

- Harold Ramis, who also helped write the movie, said he was leaning towards Don Rickles for the role of Al Czervik.

- Rodney Dangerfield played Al Czervik.

- Bill Murray said he was involved the movie because of his brother Brian.

- Jon Peters wanted Bo Derek for the role of Lacy Underall; however the other creative minds did not. The role went to Cindy Morgan.

- The film was shot at Rolling Hills, now called Grande Oaks, in Florida.

- Ramis said there were no scripted lines for Bill Murray in the whole movie; all of his lines were improvised.

- Bill Murray and Chevy Chase did not get along in real life.

- The filmmakers worked with George Lucas and his visual effects to portray the gopher.

My Take: The only other person who could have possibly played Rodney Dangerfield's role was Don Rickles, although I'm not sure it could have been done better.

Casablanca (1942)

- George Raft wanted to play the role of Richard "Rick" Blaine, which was eventually played by Humphrey Bogart.

- Joan Allison envisioned Clark Gable in the role of Rick.

- Michele Morgan was set to play the female lead of Ilsa Lund but the monetary cost was too high.

- Ingrid Bergman then played the role of Ilsa Lund.

- Hedy Lamarr was once considered for the role of Ilsa Lund.

- Hazel Scott, Lena Horne and Ella Fitzgerald were all considered for the role of a female Sam.

- The role was ultimately cast as a male character, with Dooley Wilson playing the part.

- Clarence Muse lost out on the role of Sam.

- Famed director Otto Preminger competed for the role of Major Strasser which was played by Conrad Veidt in the film.

- Joseph Cotton was also considered for the role of Victor Laszlo, which was played by Paul Henreid.

- Michael Curtiz directed and won the Academy Award for Best Director.

- The film won the Academy Award for Best Picture.

My Take: I could have seen Clark Gable as Rick. This is a great movie.

Casino Royale (2006)

- Those considered for the role of James Bond: Julian McMahon, Dominic West, Gerard Butler, Sam Worthington and Alex O'Loughlin.

- The current James Bond at the time, Pierce Brosnan, was thought to be too old to continue in the role.

- Daniel Craig won the role of James Bond.

- Henry Cavill screen tested for the part of James Bond but was considered too young for the role at the time. He plays Superman in the film Man of Steel (2013).

- Cecile DeFrance and Audrey Tauton were two other actresses up for the role of Vesper Lynd.

- Eva Green won and played the role of Vesper Lynd.

My Take: Time has shown that Daniel Craig was without a doubt the right choice. He is my second favorite Bond. I share my favorite later in the book.

Charlie and the Chocolate Factory (2005)

- Actors considered for the lead role Willy Wonka: Jim Carrey, Adam Sandler, Steve Martin, Robin Williams, Christopher Walken, Nicolas Cage, Brad Pitt, Will Smith, Mike Myers, Eric Idle, Michael Palin, Rowan Atkinson, Robert DeNiro and Michael Keaton.

- Johnny Depp played Willy Wonka in this remake of Willy Wonka and, the Chocolate Factory (1971). Gene Wilder played Willy Wonka in that film.

- Those considered for the role of Grandpa Joe: Richard Attenborough, Kirk Douglas, Albert Finney, Anthony Hopkins, Paul Newman and Christopher Lloyd.

- David Kelly eventually played Grandpa Joe.

- Sam Neill was considered to play Mr. Salt.

- James Fox played the role of Mr. Salt.

- Tim Allen, Dan Castellaneta, James Belushi, Bob Saget, Ray Romano and Ed O'Neill were all considered for the role of Mr. Teavee.

- This film was directed by Tim Burton

- Adam Godley went on to play Mr. Teavee.

- In 2003, Gregory Peck was offered the role of Grandpa Joe but he then died, this was also the case with Peter Ustinov.

My Take: Even though Johnny Depp was good, Nicholas Cage would have been my choice.

Charlie's Angels (2000)

- Angelina Jolie was originally offered the chance to take the role of Alex Munday but decided to turn it down.

- Jada Pinkett Smith also turned down the role of Alex Munday.

- Thandie Newton was cast as Alex but had to pull out due to a scheduling issue.

- Lucy Liu finally played the role of Alex Munday in the film.

- Milla Jovovich, Alyssa Milano and Julia Roberts were actresses considered for the roles of Natalie Cook, Dylan Sanders and Alex Munday.

- Jenny McCarthy did audition for the role of Natalie Cook.

- Cameron Diaz played Natalie Cook in the film.

- Drew Barrymore took the role of Dylan Sanders.

- Jordan Ladd, daughter of onetime Charlie's Angel television star Cheryl Ladd, was asked to audition for one of the angel roles but she declined the offer.

My Take: Angelina Jolie would have been the best choice and she would have elevated the film.

Cinderella Man (2005)

- Actors considered for the lead role of real life boxer James Braddock: Billy Bob Thornton, Mark Wahlberg and Clive Owen.

- Russell Crowe played the role of James Braddock.

Code of Silence (1985)

- Clint Eastwood and Kris Kristofferson both turned down the role of Eddie Cusack.

- Chuck Norris played the lead role of Eddie Cusack.

My Take: He's Chuck Norris, is there anything else that needs to be said? Actually, in case he reads this, he's Mr. Chuck Norris. Is that better Mr. Norris? Sir.

Copland (1997)

- John Travolta, Tom Hanks and Tom Cruise were among those considered for the role of Sheriff Freddy Heflin.

- Sylvester Stallone played Sheriff Freddy Heflin to critical acclaim.

- Ray Liotta wanted to have the role of Sheriff Freddie Heflin.

- Sylvester Stallone wanted to play the role of Gary "Figgsy" Figgis.

- Ray Liotta played Gary "Figgsy" Figgis.

My Take: I've already said it, Stallone rules. A very underrated film.

Death Wish (1974)

- Charles Bronson played the lead character Paul Kersey, his box office breakthrough role, which came at age fifty-two.

- Frank Sinatra was offered the lead role, accepted it, however he then decided to pull out.

- Clint Eastwood was offered the lead role after his success playing Dirty Harry; he declined the role but did suggest Gregory Peck.

- Writer Brian Garfield said originally Sidney Lumet was to direct the film with Jack Lemmon in the lead role of Paul Kersey and Henry Fonda as the police chief.

- Michael Winner directed Death Wish.

- Charles Bronson went on to make four more Death Wish movies.

My Take: Eastwood is always good and Frank Sinatra is called the Chairman of the Board for a reason. That said, no one could have played the lead role of Paul Kersey better then Charles Bronson. One of America's most underappreciated actors.

Deliverance (1972)

- Turner Classic Movies Channel said Director John Boorman wanted Marlon Brando to play the role of Lewis and Lee Marvin in the role of Ed.
- Burt Reynolds played the role of Lewis in what is considered one of his finest performances.
- Jon Voight played the role of Ed in the film.
- Charlton Heston said he turned down the role of Lewis due to his schedule.
- Henry Fonda also said he turned down the role of Lewis.
- Both the Film and the Director were nominated for Academy Awards in their respective categories.

Demolition Man (1993)

- Sylvester Stallone replaced Lori Petty in the role of Lenina Huxley with Sandra Bullock because he felt no chemistry with Petty. This change is said to have been the catalyst for Bullock ultimately getting her breakthrough role in Speed (1994).

- Sylvester Stallone wanted Jackie Chan to play Simon Phoenix but he declined the offer.

- Wesley Snipes went on to play Simon Phoenix.

- Steven Seagal and Jean Claude Van Damme were both the original choices for the lead roles of John Spartan and Simon Phoenix. Each actor wanted to play John Spartan.

- Sylvester Stallone played the role of John Spartan.

My Take: Seagal and Van Damme would have still made this an entertaining movie. It is just better with Stallone.

Die Hard (1988)

- Bruce Willis played the lead character Lt. John McClane, this was his motion picture star making role. He has starred in four Die Hard sequels.

- Robert DeNiro was offered the lead role but he turned it down.

- Tom Berenger also declined the lead role.

- Sylvester Stallone was considered for Lt. John McClane.

- Burt Reynolds was also under consideration for the lead role.

- Mel Gibson, Don Johnson, Harrison Ford, Arnold Schwarzenegger and Richard Dean Anderson (star of the television show MacGyver) were all considered for the lead.

- John McTiernan directed this movie, which changed the course of action movies.

My Take: Mel Gibson, Burt and Stallone would have been great. This film is a career maker though and it was wise to cast someone who was not an established motion picture star. Bruce Willis was a great choice. With that description, the other interesting choice would have been Don Johnson. He is a very good actor and had a similar resume to Bruce Willis at the time.

Dirty Harry (1971)

- Clint Eastwood played the lead character, Inspector Harry Callahan in this film, performing all his own stunts.

- Frank Sinatra was the first choice to play Inspector Callahan by Warner Brothers Studio. He was interested in the role but for various reasons decided to turn the role down.

- Marlon Brando was considered by Warner Brother's studio for the lead; however he was never formally contacted.

- John Wayne said he turned down the lead role, which was said to have been originally written for him. Turner Classic Movie Channel said that John Wayne's decision was one reason why he filmed the movie Brannigan (1975). That film is the only time He played a policeman in his fifty year acting career.

- Robert Mitchum said he turned down the lead role.

- Burt Lancaster claimed he turned down the lead.

- James Caan was considered for the role of Charles "Scorpio Killer" Davis which was played by Andrew Robinson. Robinson was suggested by Eastwood.

- Paul Newman was offered the lead role by Warner Bros. he decided to turn down the role and suggested Clint Eastwood.

- Directors Irvin Kershner and Sydney Pollack were wanted by Warner Bros. While Frank Sinatra was attached to the film Irvin Kershner was chosen to direct. When Sinatra dropped out so did Kershner.

- The film was directed by Don Siegel, who wanted real life war hero and actor Audie Murphy to play the role of "Scorpio" going as far as to offer him the role. Murphy was killed in a 1971 plane crash.

- The original title of this film was Dead Right.

My Take: Clint Eastwood made this role his own and it would be hard to think of anyone else playing the role and certainly not better. Frank Sinatra would have done well and of course this material has John Wayne written all over it. Those two and Charles Bronson are about it. However this was Eastwood at his best and he owns it.

The Doors (1991)

- Those considered over the years to play the real life role of Jim Morrison: Tom Cruise, Jason Patric, John Travolta and Ian Astbury (lead singer of the band The Cult).

- Val Kilmer played Jim Morrison in the film.

My Take: You only have to watch the film to know Val Kilmer was best for the role. He also did his own singing.

Dr. No (1962)

- Sean Connery played James Bond, the first actor to play this legendary character.

- The role of James Bond, in this initial film, was first offered to Cary Grant however he would only agree to star in one film. The studio wanted a much longer commitment.

- James Mason was approached after Grant however he would only commit to the role for two movies.

- Also considered for the role of James Bond were Steve Reeves who declined the role, Trevor Howard, Rex Harrison, Richard Burton, famous director John Frankenheimer and Roger Moore.

- Roger Moore eventually would take over the role of James Bond from Sean Connery, starring in his first Bond film in 1973. He would play the super spy in a record seven official films.

My Take: Cary Grant was still a huge star and would have been a good Bond. Sean Connery by any standard was fantastic as Bond.

Dumb and Dumber (1994)

- Steve Martin and Martin Short were said to be under consideration for the role of Lloyd Christmas.

- Jim Carrey played Lloyd Christmas.

- Rob Lowe was up for the role of Lloyd.

- Nicholas Cage was the first choice for the character Harry Dunne.

- Jeff Daniels played Harry Dunne.

- Gary Oldman was the original choice to play Lloyd Christmas.

My Take: Cage instead of Daniels would have made a hilarious movie even better.

Easter Parade (1948)

- Gene Kelly was originally supposed to play the character Don Hewes but he was hurt and suggested his friend Fred Astaire for the role.
- Fred Astaire did play the role of Don Hewes.
- Judy Garland played the female lead of Hannah Brown.
- Cyd Charisse was set to play the role of Nadine Hale but she got hurt.
- Ann Miller then played the role of Nadine.

My Take: Watch the movie and you will know why no one could have done better then Fred Astaire or Judy Garland.

The Expendables (2010)

- Sylvester Stallone wrote, directed and starred in the film.

- Wesley Snipes was offer the role of Hale Caeser; he was unable to take the role due to tax problems with the IRS. The role went through a rewrite so that Forest Whitaker could play the role. Whitaker eventually dropped out due to a conflict in his schedule.

- Terry Crews played Hale Caeser.

- Robert DeNiro, Al Pacino and Ben Kingsley were all considered for the role of James Munroe.

- Eric Roberts played James Munroe.

- Scott Adkins was offered the role of Dan Paine.

- Steve Austin played Dan Paine.

- Steven Seagal was approached about a role in the film but he declined.

- Jean-Claude Van Damme declined a role in the movie.

- Arnold Schwarzenegger was first offered the role of Mr. Church but wanted to have a smaller role.

- Kurt Russell was then offered the role of Mr. Church but turned it down.

- Bruce Willis who was previously making the movie Cop Out (2010) became available and played the role of Mr. Church.

- Charisma Carpenter was told to try out for the role of Lacy by Julie Benz who played the female lead in Rambo (2008).

- Charisma Carpenter won the role and played Lacy in the film.

- Mickey Rourke said he took the role of Tool because Stallone gave him a break by giving him a big role in the film Get Carter (2000).

- This is the first film that featured Hollywood titans Sylvester Stallone, Arnold Schwarzenegger and Bruce Willis together.

My Take: For the role of Lacy they needed to cast someone that did not just look good but was unique, beautiful and could act. For me, two women came to mind, Charisma Carpenter and Nadia Bjorlin, these two should be in more movies. Wonder Woman? They got it right by choosing one of them, as Charisma showed, although her role could have had more screen time here and in The Expendables 2 (2012). I would have liked a smaller cast which

Means more of the main action stars, which we got, along with Chuck Norris, I mean Mr. Chuck Norris, in The Expendables 2 (2012). Female wrestler Jamie Szantyr (Velvet Sky) would have been good in an additional female role in either film.

The Exorcist (1973)

- Audrey Hepburn, Jane Fonda, Shirley Maclaine and Anne Bancroft were all approached to play Chris MacNeil, which was eventually played by Ellen Burstyn.

- Geraldine Page declined the role of Chris.

- Jill Clayburgh auditioned for Sharon which was played by Kitty Winn.

- Stacy Keach was the first choice for the role of Fr. Karras, played in the film by Jason Miller.

- Gene Hackman was considered for the part of Fr. Karras.

- The movie studio wanted to have Marlon Brando as Fr. Merrin; Director William Friedkin objected because he thought there would be too much attention on Brando instead of the movie.

- Jack Nicholson was up to play the role of Fr. Karras.

- Kay Lenz was offered the role of Regan, played by Linda Blair however she declined because she felt she was not the right age at the time.

- Panorama Magazine said Brooke Shields was considered for Regan but Friedkin thought she was too young.

- Variety Magazine said Carrie Fisher was up for the role of Regan and that her mother Debbie Reynolds was up for the role of Chris.

Fast and Furious (2001)

- Christian Bale and Mark Wahlberg were both considered for the role of Brian O'Conner.

- Paul Walker played Brian O'Conner.

- Natalie Portman, Sarah Michelle Gellar, Kirsten Dunst, Bijou Phillips and Jessica Biel all auditioned for the role of Mia Toretto.

- Jordana Brewster played Mia Toretto.

- There have been a total of six 'Fast' films in the series.

My Take: The series has been a success and word is there will be a seventh film, so they are making good decisions.

Fast Times at Ridgemont High (1982)

- Nicholas Cage auditioned for the role of Brad Hamilton but the film studio thought he was not right for the role.
- Tom Hanks was also considered for the role of Brad.
- Judge Reinhold did play Brad Hamilton.
- Jodie Foster was considered for the role of Stacy Hamilton, she was not interested because she was committed to attending Yale at the time.
- Melanie Griffith and Tatum O'Neal were also considered for the role of Stacy.
- Diane Lane did audition for the role of Stacy.
- Brooke Shields and Ellen Barkin were both rumored to have turned down the role of Stacy.
- Jennifer Jason Leigh played Stacy Hamilton.

- Eric Stoltz auditioned to play the role of Jeff Spicoli.

- Sean Penn played Jeff Spicoli.

- Ralph Macchio was asked to play some role but his salary request was too expensive.

- Justine Bateman was offered the role of Linda Barrett however she declined so she could be in the television pilot episode for Family Ties (1982).

- Phoebe Cates played Linda Barrett.

My Take: Like some other films of the genre the cast is what helped the theme of the film come out. This film touched on some serious subjects for a comedy.

Ferris Bueller's Day Off (1986)

- John Cusack, Michael J. Fox, Rob Lowe, Jim Carrey, Johnny Depp, Tom Cruise and Robert Downey Jr. were all considered for the role of Ferris Bueller.

- The character of Ferris Bueller was played by Matthew Broderick.

Casting Call

- Anthony Michael Hall declined the role of Ferris, fearing that he was being typecast.

- Eric Stoltz auditioned for the role of Ferris Bueller.

- Emilio Estevez turned down the role of Cameron Frye which was eventually played by Alan Buck.

- John Candy auditioned for the role of Cameron but was thought to be older then the role called for.

- Paul Gleason, who played school official Richard Vernon in The Breakfast Club (1985), was considered for the role of Principal Ed Rooney, played by Jeffrey Jones.

- Ellen Barkin, Kim Basinger, Jamie Lee Curtis, Geena Davis, Carrie Fisher, Melanie Griffith, Mary Gross, Linda Hamilton, Daryl Hannah, Holly Hunter, Jessica Lange, Kelly Le Brock, Kay Lenz, Julia Louis –Dreyfus, Madonna, Catherine O'Hara, Kelly McGillis, Michelle Pfeiffer, Cybill Shepard, Meg Tilly, Sigourney Weaver, Jodie Foster, Sharon Stone and Debra Winger, were all considered for the role of Jeanie Bueller which was eventually played by Jennifer Grey.

My Take: Learn from Anthony Michael Hall's mistake, sometimes being typecast is good. Emilio Estevez should have accepted and probably wishes he did.

First Blood (1982)

- Sylvester Stallone played the lead character John Rambo.

- Richard Crenna played Colonel Sam Troutman.

- Brian Dennehy played Sheriff Walt Teasle.

- James Garner turned down the lead role of John Rambo.

- Michael Douglas also declined the lead role.

- Clint Eastwood, Al Pacino, Dustin Hoffman, John Travolta, Nick Nolte, Kris Kristofferson, Jeff Bridges and Robert DeNiro were all considered for the lead.

- Kirk Douglas was all set to play Colonel. Sam Troutman however a creative dispute arose and he pulled out of the role.

- The movie studio also considered Lee Marvin for the role of Colonel Sam Troutman.

- The movie studio had Gene Hackman under consideration for the role of Sheriff Walt Teasle.

- Ted Kotcheff directed the film.

My Take: Stallone owns the role and this is a clear choice of an actor reaping success after other actor's decline a role.

Fletch (1985)

- Gregory MacDonald author of the Fletch books, had final casting approval for the movie.

- Burt Reynolds and Mick Jagger were wanted by the studio but were not approved by MacDonald.

- Chevy Chase played Irwin "Fletch" Fletcher.

My Take: Chevy Chase was good but Burt would have been better and Mick Jagger would have been interesting to say the least.

French Connection (1971)

- Gene Hackman played the lead character Popeye Doyle.

- Gene Hackman won the Academy Award for Best Actor.

- James Caan declined the lead role of Popeye Doyle.

- Peter Boyle also turned down the lead role.

- Robert Mitchum said he turned down the lead role as well.

- Lee Marvin turned down the lead role.

- Jackie Gleason and Paul Newman were considered for the lead role.

- Jimmy Breslin, a New York City columnist was cast in the role of Popeye Doyle, he lasted about three weeks and was replaced.

- William Friedkin directed the film and won the Academy Award for Best Director.

- The film won the Academy Award for Best Picture.

My Take: Another role James Caan probably wishes he would have accepted. This is also an example of one actor's miss becoming another's hit. It is hard to argue when the result is an Academy Award, as it was for Gene Hackman. This is a great movie.

Friday the 13th (1980)

- Sally Field auditioned to play Alice Hardy, the role was played in the film by Adrienne King.

- Estell Parsons was the original choice for Mrs. Pamela Voorhees, which was played by Betsy Palmer.

From Here to Eternity (1953)

- Eli Wallach accepted to play the role of Pvt. Angelo Maggio, he then changed his mind due to his schedule.

- Frank Sinatra played Pvt. Angelo Maggio.

- Frank Sinatra won the Academy Award for Best Supporting Actor, which marked a major comeback for him as an actor.

- It is said that Sinatra's then wife, actress Ava Gardner was instrumental in convincing Columbia Studios chief Harry Cohn to hire Sinatra for the role. Sinatra was paid a small amount of eight thousand dollars for the role.

- Joan Fontaine was offered the role of Karen Holmes but declined.

- Deborah Kerr played Karen Holmes.

- Shelley Winters turned down the role of Alma.

- Donna Reed played the role of Alma.

- Donna Reed won the Academy Award for Best Supporting Actress.

- Ronald Reagan and Walter Matthau were both considered for the role of Sergeant Milton Warden.

- Burt Lancaster played Sergeant Milton Warden.

- Columbia Studios wanted Rita Hayworth to play the role of Karen Holmes.

- Tyrone Power said no to the role of Sgt. Milton Warden.

- Joan Crawford was cast as Karen but was too demanding on the set and was replaced.

- Fred Zinnemann directed and won the Academy Award for Best Director.

- The film won the Academy Award for Best Picture.

My Take: Here it is again, Shelley Winters says no, Donna Reed says yes and wins an Academy Award. It was also nice to see Frank Sinatra make his Academy Award winning comeback.

The Fugitive (1993)

- Jon Voight and Gene Hackman were both offered the role of Samuel Gerard.

- Tommy Lee Jones played Samuel Gerard and won the Academy Award for Best Supporting Actor.

- Kevin Costner and Michael Douglas were once considered for the lead role of Dr. Richard Kimble.

- Alec Baldwin was the top choice to play Dr. Kimble but eventually dropped out.

- Andy Garcia was then considered for the role of Dr. Kimble.

- Harrison Ford played Dr. Richard Kimble.

- Richard Jordan was originally cast as Dr. Nichols but was ultimately replaced by Jeroen Krabbe.

- The first director Walter Hill, (48hrs, 1982) who eventually pulled out of the film, wanted Nick Nolte for the lead role but Nolte said no.
- Andrew Davis took over and directed the film.

My Take: Tommy Lee Jones gets a role others turned down and wins an Academy Award. Jon Voight and Gene Hackman have some consolation as they each had already won Best Actor Academy Awards and are still considered two of the best.

Gentleman Prefer Blondes (1953)

- Betty Grable was originally wanted to play the role of Lorelei Lee.
- Judy Holliday said no to the role of Lorelei Lee.
- Marilyn Monroe did play Lorelei Lee in the movie.

Ghostbusters (1984)

- The original desired cast was: John Belushi, Dan Aykroyd, Eddie Murphy and John Candy.

- The movie was filmed with this cast: Bill Murray as Dr. Peter Venkman, Dan Aykroyd as Dr. Raymond Stantz, Harold Ramis as Dr. Egon Spengler and Rick Moranis as Louis Tully.

- Also considered for the role of Dr. Egon Spengler were Christopher Walken, John Lithgow, Christopher Lloyd and Jeff Goldblum.

- Paul Rubens a.k.a. Pee-Wee Herman turned down the role of Gozer which was played by Slavitza Jovan.

- Anne Carlisle turned down the role of the Zuul which was voiced by Ivan Reitman, who directed the film.

- Eddie Murphy filmed Beverly Hills Cop instead of taking the role of Winston Zeddmore, played by Ernie Hudson.

- Annie Potts of Designing Women television fame played the role of Janine Melnitz.

- Lyndsey Buckingham of Fleetwood Mac fame turned down an offer to write the theme song.

- Huey Lewis first turned down the opportunity to write the theme song. He then changed his mind and said he would do it.

He later sued the artist, Ray Parker Jr., who was hired to write the theme song, for plagiarism. Lewis said the title song was very similar to his hit song (I Want a New Drug, 1984), the song "Ghostbusters" was a number one hit. Huey Lewis won the lawsuit, which was settled out of court.

My Take: This movie is one of the highest grossing comedies of all time. They got it right, with Bill Murray lifting it to the next level.

Gladiator (2000)

- Mel Gibson declined the role of Maximus, played by Russell Crowe.

- Russell Crowe won the Academy Award for Best Actor for this role.

- Antonio Banderas was once considered for the role of Maximus.

- Jennifer Lopez auditioned for the role of Lucilla, which eventually went to Connie Nielson.

- The film won the Academy Award for Best Picture.

- The film was directed by Ridley Scott.

The Godfather (1972)

- Marlon Brando played the lead role of Vito Corleone.

- Marlon Brando won his second Academy Award for Best Actor.

- Paramount Pictures considered Ernest Borgnine, Edward G. Robinson, Orson Welles, Danny Thomas, Richard Conte and Anthony Quinn for role of Vito Corleone.

- Burt Lancaster wanted the role of Vito Corleone but was never considered.

- Director Francis Ford Coppola wanted Laurence Olivier or Marlon Brando as Vito.

- Frank Sinatra had discussions about the role of Vito and even offered to play the role but Coppola insisted on Brando.

- Sylvester Stallone auditioned for the roles Paulie Gatto which was played by John Martino and Carlo Rizzi which was played by Gianni Russo.

- Frankie Avalon and Vic Damone both auditioned for the role of Johnny Fontane, however Coppola gave the role to Vic Damone. The producers of the film overruled Coppola and gave the role to Al Martino.

- Olivia Hussey was considered for the role of Apollonia. Coppola wanted Stefania Sandrelli but she said no.

- James Caan was not the original choice for the role of Sonny Corleone, he took the role over from Carmine Carridi.

- Burt Reynolds was also considered for the role of Sonny Corleone.

- Martin Sheen and Dean Stockwell both auditioned for the role of Michael Corleone.

- Rod Stieger wanted the role of Michael but he was considered too old at the time.

- Warren Beatty, Jack Nicholson and Dustin Hoffman were all offered the role of Michael Corleone but each of them turned the role down.

- Alain Delon and Burt Reynolds were both suggested for the role of Michael Corleone, however Coppola decided against both.

- Ryan O'Neal was considered for the role of Michael.

- Producer Robert Evans wanted Robert Redford to play the role of Michael.

- Robert DeNiro auditioned for the characters Michael and Sonny Corleone and was almost cast as Carlo. He was then cast as Paulie but had to back out due to his schedule.

- Al Pacino played Michael Corleone.

- Jerry Van Dyke, Bruce Dern, Paul Newman and James Caan all auditioned for the role of Tom Hagen.

- Robert Duvall played Tom Hagen.

- Andy Griffith was almost chosen to play Vito Corleone.

- The film won the Academy Award for Best Picture.

My take: Burt Reynolds would have been excellent as Sonny. There is no one who could have played Vito better then Marlon Brando. The actors did a very good job in this film.

Goldeneye (1995)

- Mel Gibson, Liam Neeson, Sam Neill and Hugh Grant were all rumored to be in the running for the role of James Bond.

- Pierce Brosnan won the role and played James Bond.

- Paulina Porizkova and Eva Herzigova were both offered the role of Natalya Simonova but each of them declined.

- Izabella Scorupco played Natalya Simonova.

- The Rolling Stones were offered the opportunity to sing the title song, but declined.

- U2 wrote the title song, while Tina Turner performed it.

- The script was written with the previous James Bond, Timothy Dalton still in mind as 007.

- This was the last movie viewed by Albert R. Broccoli, longtime James Bond producer.

- The role of Alex Trevelyan was played by Sean Bean.

- Producers wanted Anthony Hopkins for the role of Alex however he turned the role down.

- Alan Rickman also declined the role of Alex Trevelyan.

- This was the first James Bond movie produced by current Bond producers Barbara Broccoli, daughter of Albert and her half brother Michael G. Wilson.

- The six year gap from the release of the previous Bond film is the longest in the history of the series.

My Take: Possibly the most difficult role in film history to recast even when necessary. This was a solid choice and it showed at the box office. You will read later that Brosnan was almost Bond the previous time it was recast. Mel Gibson would have been an interesting choice as an Australian, after all Sean Connery is Scottish not English.

Gone With the Wind (1939)

- Clark Gable played the lead character Rhett Butler.

- Vivian Leigh played the female lead character Scarlett, she won the Academy Award for Best Actress.

- These actresses were considered for the role of Scarlett: Lucille Ball, Bette Davis, Barbara Stanwyck, Jean Arthur, Claudette Colbert, Joan Crawford, Paulette Goddard, Katharine Hepburn, Olivia de Havilland, Carol Lombard, Norma Shearer, Tallulah Bankhead and Margaret Sullivan. Tallulah was a real "southern belle" and considered the favorite. Her personal life made the producers uneasy about hiring her.

- Gary Cooper turned down the lead role, saying "Gone with the Wind is going to be the biggest flop in Hollywood history." "I'm just glad it will be Clark Gable who's falling on his face and not Gary Cooper."

- When adjusted for ticket price inflation by various sources, Gone with the Wind is the highest grossing movie of all time, with a gross in the billions, depending on the source.

Casting Call

- Errol Flynn and Ronald Coleman were the only other actors considered for the role of Rhett by producer David O. Selznick.

- Margaret Mitchell, author of Gone with the Wind, wanted Basil Rathbone, who was famous for his portrayal of Sherlock Holmes, to play Rhett Butler.

- Hattie McDaniel played the role of Mammy. She won the Academy Award for Best Supporting Actress, becoming the first black American to be nominated and to win an Academy Award.

- Clark Gable was so angry that Hattie McDaniel would not be able to attend the premiere in racially segregated Atlanta that he threatened not to attend unless she could also go. The only reason he went, McDaniel herself convinced him to go.

- Melvyn Douglas, Vincent Price, Robert Young, Douglas Fairbanks Jr. and Ray Milland all auditioned for the role of Ashley Wilkes.

- Pricilla Lane was considered for the role of Melanie Wilkes.

- Judy Garland was the favorite for the role of Carreen, Scarlett's sister. Garland was busy filming The Wizard of Oz (1939)

- Victor Fleming directed the film and won the Academy Award for Best Director.

- George Cukor and Sam Wood have uncredited director roles.

- The film won the Academy Award for Best Picture and has the longest running time of any film to win the award.

My Take: The most financially successful film ever says it all. The only issue I have is I think Clark Gable should have won the Academy Award for Best Actor.

The Graduate (1967)

- Robert Redford and Lee Stanley both tested for the lead role of Benjamin Braddock.

- Dustin Hoffman played Benjamin Braddock.

- Greyson Hall was considered for the role of Mrs. Robinson.

- Ann Bancroft played Mrs. Robinson.

- Charles Grodin was cast as Benjamin Braddock but a disagreement over his salary caused him to drop out.

- Mike Nichols directed and won the Academy Award for Best Director.

- Nichols approached Ava Gardner for the role of Mrs. Robinson and he also wanted French actress Jeanne Moreau for the part.

- Doris Day said she was offered the role of Mrs. Robinson but declined.

- Judy Garland was considered for the role of Mrs. Robinson.

- Warren Beatty was up to play the role of Benjamin Braddock.

- Patricia Neal was considered for Mrs. Robinson but said no, this was allegedly due to health reasons.

- Burt Ward (Robin, of the television show Batman) turned down the lead role, 20th Century Fox Studios also said no to him playing the role.

- Dustin Hoffman says Gene Hackman was given the role of Mr. Robinson and then fired.

- Marty Hamilton played Mr. Robinson.

- Patty Duke was offered the role of Elaine Robinson but declined.

- Williams Daniels, Jack Nicholson and Ronald Reagan were all considered for the role of Mr. Braddock.

- William Daniels played Mr. Braddock.

- Sally Field tested for the role of Elaine.

- Susan Hayward said no to the part of Mrs. Robinson.

- Candace Bergan auditioned for Elaine.

- Natalie Wood was offered the role of Elaine Robinson, played by Katherine Ross, but decided not to accept.

Grease (1978)

- Henry Winkler (the Fonz, from the television show Happy Days) declined the lead role of Danny Zuko.

- John Travolta played the role of Danny Zuko.

- Susan Dey (from television's The Partridge Family) said no to the role of Sandy Olsson.

- Olivia Newton-John played the role of Sandy Olsson.

- Carrie Fisher was considered for the role of Betty Rizzo.

- Stockard Channing played Betty Rizzo.

The Greatest Story Ever Told (1965)

- Director George Stevens originally wanted Richard Burton to play Jesus.

- Max Von Sydow played Jesus.

- Alec Guiness was wanted for a cameo.

- Telly Savalas, who played Pontius Pilate, shaved his head bald for the role and kept it bald the rest of his life.

My Take: It is hard to cast the role of Jesus and to make a film about Him. This was well done on both counts.

Groundhog Day (1993)

- Director Harold Ramis considered Chevy Chase, Steve Martin, John Travolta and Tom Hanks for the role of Phil Conners. He thought they were too nice compared to Bill Murray, who played the role.

- Singer Tori Amos was considered for the role of Rita.

- Andie MacDowell played the role of Rita.

Halloween (1978)

- Christopher Lee (Scalamenger from James Bond's The Man with the Golden Gun 1974) said no to the role of Dr. Sam Loomis.

- Donald Pleasance played the role of Dr. Sam Loomis.

- Ann Lockhart was Director John Carpenter's first choice to play Laurie Strode.

- Jamie Lee Curtis, daughter of Tony Curtis and Janet Leigh, played Laurie Strode.

- Dennis Quaid was wanted to play Bob Simms but his schedule would not allow.

- John Michael Graham played the role of Bob Simms.

Heat (1995)

- Among those considered for the lead roles of Lt. Vincent Hanna and Neil McCauley were Nick Nolte and Jeff Bridges.

- Al Pacino played Lt. Vincent Hanna.

- Robert DeNiro played Neil McCauley.

- Kris Kristofferson was considered for the role of Nate.

- Jon Voight played the role of Nate.

- Don Johnson was considered for the role of Michael Cheritto and as a back-up for the roles played by Al Pacino and Robert DeNiro.

- Jean-Claude Van Dam was briefly considered for the role of Michael Cheritto.

- Michael Madsen cast as Michael but was then replaced.

- Tom Sizemore played Michael Cheritto.

- Keanu Reeves was signed for the role of Chris Shiherlis.

- Val Kilmer was then given the role of Chris Shiherlis, which he played.

My Take: Don Johnson would have been great as either lead.

High Noon (1952)

- The lead role of Marshal Will Kane was offered to Gregory Peck, Charleston Heston and Marlon Brando all of whom said no.

- Gary Cooper played the role of Marshal Will Kane and won his second Academy Award for Best Actor.

- Lee van Cleef, who was famous for starring in westerns, was cast as Deputy Harvey Pell.

- Lloyd Bridges played the role of Deputy Harvey Pell.

My Take: This one is very unique, all three actors listed who turned down the role were already or eventually would be Academy Award Best Actor winners. Another Academy Award winner accepts and wins again.

His Girl Friday (1940)

- Howard Hawks was the director of the film.

- Clark Gable was thought to be the best choice for the lead role of Walter Burns.

- Cary Grant eventually played Walter Burns.

- Jean Arthur was the first choice to play Hildy Johnson but she said no due to a strained working relationship with director Howard Hawks.

- Ginger Rogers, Carole Lombard, Claudette Colbert and Irene Dunne all turned down the role of Hildy, which was then played by Rosalind Russell.

Home Alone (1990)

- The role of Uncle Frank, played by Gerry Bamman, was written for Kelsey Grammer.

- Robert DeNiro turned down the role of Harry, which was played by Joe Pesci.

- Sigourney Weaver, Diane Keaton, Holly Hunter, Jodie Foster, Geena Davis, Glenn Close, Jamie Lee Curtis, Stockard Channing, Carrie Fisher, Kelly McGillis, Linda Hamilton, Helen Hunt, Laura Dern, Anjelica Huston, Sharon Stone, Michelle Pfeiffer, Jessica Lange, Daryl Hannah, Debra Winger and Annie Potts were all considered for the role of Kate McCallister which was played by Catherine O'Hara.

- Michael Douglas, Martin Sheen, Kevin Costner, Dan Aykroyd, John Travolta, Tom Skerritt, Bill Murray, James Belushi, Chevy Chase, Harrison Ford, Mel Gibson, Sylvester Stallone, Rick Moranis, Dennis Quaid and Jack Nicholson were considered to play the role of Peter McCallister, which was played by John Heard.

- The idea for the film has its foundation in the kitchen scene from Uncle Buck (1989), which took place between John Candy and Macaulay Culkin.

- The role of Kevin McCallister was written for Macaulay Culkin. The director Chris Columbus auditioned hundreds of other boys to make sure Culkin was the right choice. Culkin did play Kevin.

My Take: Kelsey Grammer would have been better as Uncle Frank. This film was a great success, so there is not much to take a second look at.

The Hunt for Red October (1990)

- Kevin Costner was the original choice to play Jack Ryan.

- Alec Baldwin played Jack Ryan (Harrison Ford replaced Baldwin as Jack Ryan in Patriot Games 1992).

- Harrison Ford turned down the role of Jack Ryan for this film.

- Klaus Maria Brandauer was originally cast as Marko Ramius however he broke his leg before filming began. He then suggested his friend Sean Connery for the role.

- Sean Connery played Marko Ramius after initially turning it down.

- Director John McTiernan had to pass up the opportunity to direct the sequel to his hit film Die Hard (1988) due to his obligations to this film. Renny Harlin went on to direct that sequel, Die Hard 2 (1990).

The Hustler (1961)

- Jack Lemmon declined the role of "Fast" Eddie Felson.

- Cliff Robertson lost the "Fast" Eddie Felson role to Paul Newman.

- On the Larry King show Kim Novak said she turned down the Sarah Packard role.

- Piper Laurie played Sarah Packard.

- Bobby Darin was given the lead role after Paul Newman had an issue with his schedule. That issue was cleared up and the role was given back to him (Elizabeth Taylor was held up filming Cleopatra which delayed the filming of Seesaw which was also to star Paul Newman).

- That delay made Paul Newman once again available to film The Hustler.

Interview with the Vampire (1994)

- Author Ann Rice, who wrote the book of the same title, said she wrote the part of Lestat de Lioncourt with Rutger Hauer in mind.

- John Travolta was chosen play Lestat at one point.

- Johnny Depp was offered at one time, the role of Lestat.

- Jeremy Irons turned down the role of Lestat.

- Tom Cruise, much to the dismay of Ann Rice, played the role of Lestat de Lioncourt. Upon viewing a screening she was pleased enough with his performance.

- Evan Rachel Wood, Christina Ricci, Dominique Swain, Erin Moore and Julia Stiles all auditioned for the role of Claudia.

- Kirsten Dunst played Claudia.

- River Phoenix was originally set to play Daniel Malloy. He died from a drug overdose before he could play the role.

- Christian Slater played Daniel Malloy.

- Neil Jordan directed.

My Take: Rutger Hauer or Jeremy Irons would have added a more polished feel to the film visually. It is always sad when a young person loses their life in any way and in this case needlessly to drugs, actor or not.

Iron Man (2008)

- Nicholas Cage and Tom Cruise were both interested in the lead role of Tony Stark/Iron man.

- Clive Owen and Sam Rockwell were under consideration for the lead.
- Robert Downey Jr. played Tony Stark/Iron man.
- Rachel McAdams was offered the role of Pepper Potts but she declined.
- Gwyneth Paltrow played the role of Pepper Potts.
- Timothy Olyphant also read for the lead.
- There have been three Iron Man films.
- Robert Downey Jr. has played Iron Man/Tony Stark four times, one of those was in the film The Avengers (2012).

My Take: In addition to Robert Downey Jr. owning this role, it is a feel good story the way he has improved himself, which makes him a success at what is important, life. Another movie that I think Nadia Bjorlin or Charisma Carpenter were right for.

It Happened One Night (1934)

- Robert Montgomery turned down the lead role of Peter Warne, believing the script was the worst thing he had ever read.

- This movie won the Academy Award for Best Writing/Screenplay.

- Clark Gable played the role of Peter Warne.

- Clark Gable won the Academy Award for Best Actor.

- Myrna Loy and Constance Bennett both said no to the role of Ellie Andrews. Myrna Loy said no because she thought the film would be a failure.

- Claudette Colbert played the role of Ellie Andrews and won the Academy Award for Best Actress..

- Frank Capra (It's a Wonderful Life 1946) directed and won the Academy Award for Best Director.

- The film won the Academy Award for Best Picture.

- This film was the first Academy Award Best Picture winner to also win the Best Actor and Best Actress award.

- It was the first of only three motion pictures to win all five major Academy Awards.

My Take: I find it amazing that one of the most decorated films of all time and the first, was released nearly 80 years ago.

It's a Wonderful Life (1946)

- The lead role of George Bailey which was played by James Stewart, was originally written with Cary Grant in mind.

- Lionel Barrymore, who played Mr. Potter, helped convince James Stewart to take the role.

- Vincent Price was also considered for the role of Mr. Potter.

- Ginger Rogers and Jean Arthur were the top choices to play Mary Hatch Bailey.

- The role of Mary Hatch Bailey was played by Donna Reed.

My Take: Nothing to say in regards to the casting. I will say this has the best message because it is true to real life. Every life touches those that come in contact with that life. In this movie George Bailey needs to be reminded by God. One of the best feel good movies of all time.

Jaws (1975)

- Steven Spielberg wanted Sterling Hayden to play the role of Sam Quint.

- Robert Shaw was cast as Sam Quint, even though he had issues with the IRS.

- Charlton Heston was considered for the role of Chief Martin Brody.

- Roy Scheider played Chief Martin Brody.

- Jeff Bridges, Timothy Bottoms, Jon Voight and Jan-Michael Vincent were all considered for the role of Matt Hooper.

- Richard Dreyfuss played Matt Hooper.

- Victoria Principal was under consideration for the role of Ellen Brody.

- Lorraine Gary played Ellen Brody.

- Steven Spielberg considered Lee Marvin for the role of Sam Quint but he declined the role.

- Steven Spielberg offered the role of Chief Brody to Robert Duvall who said no because it was to "visible" a role.

- The author of Jaws, Peter Benchley wanted to have Robert Redford and/or Paul Newman in the lead role.

My Take: Roy Scheider was great, Duvall should have accepted, Victoria Principal would have been perfect for the role of Ellen.

Judge Dredd (1995)

- Arnold Schwarzenegger was considered early on for the lead role of Joseph "Judge" Dredd.

- Sylvester Stallone played Judge Dredd.

- Joe Pesci turned down the role of Herman "Fergie" Ferguson, which was played by Rob Schneider.

- Christopher Walken turned down the role of Rico.

- Armand Assante played Rico.

Jurassic Park (1993)

- William Hurt turned down the role of Dr. Alan Grant without ever reading the script.

- Harrison Ford also turned down the role of Dr. Alan Grant.

- Sam Neill played Dr. Alan Grant.

- Tim Burton, Richard Donner and Joe Dante were all considered to direct the film.

- Steven Spielberg directed.

- George Lucas handled the post production of the film.

- Juliette Binoche was offered the role of Dr. Ellie Sattler but turned it down.

- Laura Dern played Dr. Ellie Sattler.

- Brian Cox was interviewed for the role of Robert Muldoon, played by Bob Peck.

Laura (1944)

- The original choice for the title role of Laura was Jennifer Jones but she declined.

- Gene Tierney played Laura.

- Hedy Lamarr was also offered the role of Laura but said no.

- The theme song was written by David Raskin. It was originally titled "Judy" in honor of Judy Garland but was eventually changed to Laura.

Lawrence of Arabia (1962)

- Marlon Brando signed on as the lead role of T.E. Lawrence, but later dropped out.

- Albert Finney also turned down the lead.

- Cary Grant, Alan Ladd, Burgess Meredith, Robert Donat and Lawrence Olivier were all considered for the lead role.

- Alec Guinness wanted to play the lead but was thought to be too old, he then accepted the role of Prince Feisal when Lawrence Olivier turned it down.

- Sam Spiegel wanted Cary Grant to play General Allenby but he was talked out of it.

- Katherine Hepburn wanted Peter O'Toole to play Lawrence, which he did.

- Kirk Douglas was considered for the role of Jackson Bentley.

- Edmond O'Brien was replaced as Jackson Bentley by Arthur Kennedy, who was recommended by Anthony Quinn.
- David Lean directed and won the Academy Award for Best Director.
- The film won the Academy Award for Best Picture.

My Take: David Lean is fairly unknown even with his awards, change that if you want to see some great movies.

Live and Let Die (1973)

- Sean Connery decided not to do another James Bond film, which required a search for a new James Bond.
- Roger Moore was eventually introduced as James Bond with Sean Connery's approval.
- United Artists Studios wanted an American actor to play James Bond and considered among others, Burt Reynolds, Paul Newman and Robert Redford for the role.
- Bond Producer Albert R. Broccoli suggested Roger Moore.

- Gayle Hunnicutt signed for the role of Soltaire but soon dropped out when she became pregnant.

- Diana Ross was considered for the role of Soltaire.

- Jane Seymour played Solitaire which was her first starring role.

My Take: Burt and the others would have been interesting as it would have marked an American actor playing the role. However Roger Moore was without a doubt the best choice. He had it more difficult then any of the actors who have taken over the role of James Bond. He had to follow Sean Connery and he did it better then anyone thought because he did not just take over, he made the role his own. I alluded earlier to this, Roger Moore is my favorite James Bond.

Live Free or Die Hard (2007)

- Justin Timberlake was in talks to play John McClane's son however the role was left out of the film.

- Jessica Simpson auditioned for the role of Lucy Gennaro McClane.

- Mary Elizabeth Winstead played Lucy.

- Director Len Wiseman wanted Scott Speedman for the role of Matt Farrell. (Scott Speedman starred in the Wiseman directed Underworld, 2003 with Kate Beckinsale, Wiseman's wife in real life)

- Bruce Willis wanted Ben Affleck for the role of Matt.

- Kal Penn auditioned for Matt.

- Justin Long played Matt Farrell.

My Take: It may have taken 12 years but this was worth the wait. This film deserves to be mentioned with the first two in the series.

The Living Daylights (1987)

- Timothy Dalton was the original choice to take over for Roger Moore but was unavailable due to his schedule. Pierce Brosnan was signed for the role and then ruled out because he couldn't get out of his contract for the Remington Steele television show. NBC took a long time to decide whether they would have another season of Remington Steele, when they finally decided on one more, Timothy Dalton had also become available. Remington Steele only shot six more episodes.

- Also considered for the role of James Bond: Sam Neill, Mel Gibson and Sean Bean.

- Timothy Dalton was offered the role of James Bond in 1969 for On Her Majesty's Secret Service however he said no, feeling that he was too young.

- Timothy Dalton also turned down the role of James Bond in Diamonds Are Forever (1971) for the same reason.

- The Studio was unsure at times of Roger Moore's future commitment, so Timothy Dalton was approached for the Bond films For Your Eyes Only (1981), Octopussy (1983) and A View to a Kill (1985).

My Take: Timothy Dalton is probably the most maligned James Bond in the history of the storied franchise. This is unfair because following Roger Moore was as difficult as following Sean Connery. In some ways more diffcult because the franchise was even more established at this point. Brosnan proved later that he could play

Bond. Mel Gibson would have been a great choice. The two films in which Timothy Dalton played Bond are entertaining films.

The Lord of the Rings (2001)

- Stuart Townsend was originally cast as Aragorn but he was replaced when Director Peter Jackson thought an older actor was needed for the role.

- Viggo Mortenson played Aragorn.

- John Astin (Gomez Addams of televisions Addams Family, 1964), auditioned for the role of Gandalf the Grey. His son Sean Astin played the role of Samwise 'Sam' Gamgee.

- Ian Mckellen played Gandalf the Grey.

- Daniel Day Lewis turned down the role of Aragorn.

- David Bowie was said to be interested in the role of Elf Lord Elrond.

- Hugo Weaving played Elf Lord Elrond.

- Orlando Bloom auditioned for a different role then the one he played which was Legolas Greenleaf.

- Tom Baker was also considered for Gandalf the Grey.

- Christopher Lee was told by J.R. Tolkein he could play Gandalf the Grey if a film was ever made. Lee wanted the role, but was instead offered the role of Saluman. He took it.

- Sam Neill was considered for the role of Gandalf the Grey.

- Russell Crowe was the top choice of Director Peter Jackson to play Aragorn. Crowe was excited but unable to take the role due to conflicts in his schedule.

- Dominic Monoghan who played Meriodac 'Merry' Brandybuck, auditioned for the role of Frodo Baggins.

- Jake Gyllenhaal also auditioned for the role of Frodo Baggins.

- Elijah Wood played Frodo Baggins.

- Ian Holm was always director Peter Jackson's first choice for the role of Bilbo Baggins, Holm played that role.

- Anthony Hopkins turned down a role in the film, which one is not known.

- Kate Winslet also turned down a role in the film.

- Jeremy Irons, Tim Curry and Malcolm McDowell were all considered by Peter Jackson for the role of Saluman even though Christopher Lee was Jackson's first choice.

- Sean Connery was offered the role of Gandolf the Grey at some point but eventually turned it down.

My Take: Russell Crowe and Sean Connery would make any film better .

The Maltese Falcon (1941)

- George Raft was offered the role Sam Spade but said no.

- Ingrid Bergman was offered the role of Brigid O'Shaughnessy.

- Mary Astor played the role of Brigid O'Shaughnessy.

- Humphrey Bogart played Samuel Spade.

Man of Steel (2013)

- Matt Bomer, Zac Efron, and Colin O'Donoghue were all considered for the lead role of Clark Kent/Superman.

- Henry Cavill won the role of Clark Kent/Superman. He also finished second to Daniel Craig for the role of James Bond in Casino Royale (2006). He was considered to young at that time.

- Natalie Portman, Anne Hathaway, Kristen Stewart, Rachel McAdams, Kristen Bell, Mary Elizabeth Winstead, Olivia Wilde, Jessica Biel and Mila Kunis were all considered for the role of Lois Lane.

- Amy Adams played Lois Lane.

- Darren Aronofsky (The Wrestler, 2008), Tony Scott and Duncan Jones were considered to direct the movie.

- Ben Affleck turned down the opportunity to direct the film.

- Zack Snyder directed the film.

- Sela Ward, Julianne Moore, Lisa Rinna, and Jodie Foster were being considered for the role of Martha Kent.

- Diane Lane played Martha Kent.

- Bruce Greenwood, Michael Biehn, Dennis Quaid and Kurt Russell were all considered for the role of Jonathan Kent.

- Kevin Costner played the role of Jonathan Kent.

- Viggo Mortensen was thought of for the role of General Zod.

- Michael Shannon played General Zod.

- Russell Crowe played the role of Jor-El, the same role Marlon Brando played in the original film.

- Christopher Nolan of Batman Begins (2005), The Dark Knight (2008), and The Dark Knight Rises (2012), helped write the story.

My Take: I think a film of this scale offers rare casting opportunities not available in many other films. Many times in cinematic history theses types of movies provide for the successful introduction of an actor or actress who is not one by trade. I think there was a chance to do that here. I would have cast real life reporter Andrea Tantaros as Lois Lane. The character of Lois Lane is a successful reporter who is very intelligent, confident and extremely attractive. In real life Andrea Tantaros fits that very description. She would have really added something unique to the film. Success is many times found by thinking outside the norm.

Manhunter (1986)

- Brian Dennehy, John Lithgow, and Mandy Patinkin were considered for the lead role of Hannibal Lektor.

- Director Michael Mann also considered fellow director William Friedkin (The French Connection, 1971) for the role of Hannibal Lektor.

- Brian Dennehy suggested Brian Cox, for the role of Hannibal Lektor.

- Brian Cox played the role of Hannibal Lektor.

- Jeff Bridges was discussed at one time for the role of FBI agent Will Graham.

- The movie studio wanted Don Johnson to play Will Graham.

- The role of Will Graham was played by William Peterson, best known for his role on television's hit show CSI (2000).

My Take: William Peterson was good. I think Don Johnson would have been even better. This is a role that was tailor made for him.

The Matrix (1999)

- Keanu Reeves played the role of Neo.

- Ewan McGregor was offered the role of Neo, instead he chose to film Star Wars: The Phantom Menace (1999).

- Leonardo DiCaprio was once considered for the role of Neo.

- Nicholas Cage declined the role of Neo for family reasons.

- Tom Cruise was also considered for Neo.

- Will Smith was approached but said no due to his filming schedule of the movie The Wild, Wild West (1999).

- Johnny Depp was thought to be a possible first choice of the directors.

- Warner Brothers Studios wanted Brad Pitt or Val Kilmer for the lead role. After they said no to the role, then Keanu Reeves was considered the next choice.

- Gary Oldman was considered for the role of Morpheus.

- Laurence Fishburne played the role of Morpheus.

- Jean Reno was approached for the role of Agent Smith but he declined choosing to take a role in the film Godzilla (1998).

- Sean Connery was originally offered the role of Morpheus, he declined the role.

My Take: I think Val Kilmer would have been the best of all the choices. Ewan saying no was a huge gain for Keanu.

Maverick (1994)

- Paul Newman was offered the role of Marshal Zane Cooper but declined.

- James Garner played the role of Marshal Zane Cooper (James Garner played the role of Bret Maverick on the television show Maverick 1957).

- Meg Ryan was the original choice for the role of Annabell Bransford.

- Jodie Foster, a personal friend of Mel Gibson, played Annabell Bransford.

- Mel Gibson played the lead role of Bret Maverick.

- Richard Donner directed (He directed Mel Gibson in Lethal Weapon 1987).

Meet the Parents (2000)

- Jim Carrey was originally supposed to play the lead role of Gaylord Greg Focker.

- Ben Stiller played Gaylord Greg Focker.

- Christopher Walken was the second choice to play the role of Jack Byrnes.

- Robert DeNiro played Jack Byrnes.

- Julia Stiles auditioned for the role of Pam Byrnes.

- Teri Polo played Pam Byrnes.

My Take: I think Christopher Walken would have been better as Jack Byrnes.

Men in Black (1997)

- Chris O'Donnell was offered the role of James Darrel Edwards III/Agent J.

- Will Smith played Agent J.

- Clint Eastwood was offered the role of Kevin Brown/Agent K and said no.

- Tommy Lee Jones played Agent K.

- David Schwimmer was offered the role of Agent J and declined.

- Bruce Campbell was offered a small role but eventually backed out.

- There have been two more successful sequels in this series.

My Take: I would like the films even more with Clint Eastwood over Tommy Lee Jones. Really bad decision by David Schwimmer.

Miami Vice (2006)

- Considered to play Sonny Crockett: Tom Cruise, Brad Pitt and Matthew McConaughey.

- Colin Farrell played Sonny Crockett.

- Edward James Olmos was offered the opportunity to reprise his role from the television show Miami Vice (1984), Lt. Martin Castillo, but he said no.

- Barry Shabako Henley played Lt. Martin Castillo.

- Don Johnson, who played Sonny Crockett on the television show, suggested Colin Farrell for his role.

My Take: I would have cast Don Johnson and Philip Michael Thomas. They could have pulled it off.

Mr. & Mrs. Smith (2005)

- Nicole Kidman was originally set to play Mrs. Jane Smith.
- Angelina Jolie played Mrs. Jane Smith.
- Johnny Depp was originally set to play Mr. John Smith but said no due to his schedule at the time.
- Brad Pitt played Mr. John Smith.
- Cate Blanchett was once considered for the female lead.
- Gwen Stefani, Eva Green and Catherine Zeta-Jones were also considered after Nicole Kidman for the female lead.

My Take: This movie ended up with the right choices. After all we may not have had Brangelina with out it.

North by Northwest (1959)

- Cary Grant played the lead character Roger Thornhill.

- Eva Marie Saint played the lead character Eve Kendall.

- James Mason played the role of Phillip Van Damm.

- James Stewart wanted to play Roger Thornhill however Director Alfred Hitchcock said no because of his age. At the time of filming Cary Grant was actually four years older then James Stewart.

- MGM Studios wanted Gregory Peck to play the lead role.

- Yul Brynner was considered for the role of Phillip Van Damm.

- MGM Studios wanted Cyd Charisse for the role of Eve Kendall; it was Director Alfred Hitchcock who really wanted Eva Marie Saint.

- William Holden was suggested as the lead but was never approached.

- Sophia Loren was considered for the character Eve Kendall however it never went anywhere due to contractual issues.

My Take: I like James Stewart a great deal however Cary Grant was excellent and Hitchcock was right, if you have not seen this film you are missing out.

The Omen (1976)

- Roy Scheider, Dick Van Dyke, William Holden and Charlton Heston all turned down the lead role of Robert Thorn which was played by Gregory Peck.

- William Holden went on to play Robert Thorn's brother, Richard in 'Damien: Omen II' (1978).

- The series concluded with the film Omen III: The Final Conflict (1981).

My Take: All of those actors are great and would have done well.

On the Waterfront (1954)

- Producer Sam Spiegel always wanted Marlon Brando to play the lead role of Terry Malloy because he was already a box office draw.

- Marlon Brando declined the role when first approached.

- Frank Sinatra then accepted the lead role.

- The role of Terry Malloy was originally written for John Garfield.

- Grace Kelly turned down the role of Edie Doyle to make the Alfred Hitchcock movie Rear Window (1954).

- The role of Edie Doyle was played by Eva Marie Saint who won the Academy Award for Best Supporting Actress.

- Elizabeth Montgomery was one of the final two choices for the role of Edie Doyle.

- Lawrence Tierney was offered the role of Charlie Malloy but his salary was too high.

- Rod Steiger played the role of Charlie Malloy.

- Marlon Brando did play Terry Malloy.

- Marlon Brando won the Academy Award for Best Actor. It was his third nomination in a row in that category and his first win.

- Elia Kazan directed and won the Academy Award for Best Director.

- The film won the Academy Award for Best Picture.

My Take: Sinatra would have done very well, however Brando won the Academy Award and was the right call.

The Pink Panther (1964)

- Peter Ustinov was offered the role of Inspector Jacque Clouseau however for reasons unknown he did not show up.

- Janet Leigh was offered the role of Simone Clouseau but she declined.

- Ava Gardner accepted the role of Simone but her "extra" requests were to demanding.

- Inspector Jacque Clouseau was played by Peter Sellers, a role he would play a total of five times.

- Simone Clouseau was played by French actress Capucine.

- Blake Edwards directed.

My Take: Peter Sellers owns this role and performed it at a very high comedic level in each film. The performances are super funny in both the dialogue and physical comedy.

Pirates of the Caribbean (2003)

- Stephen Spielberg had an interest in the film and wanted Bill Murray, Steve Martin or Robin Williams for the role of Captain Jack Sparrow, which was eventually played by Johnny Depp. Disney did not give the green light to the film.

- Michael Keaton, Jim Carrey, Christopher Walken and Cary Elwes were all considered for the role of Captain Jack Sparrow.

- Ewan McGregor, Tobey Maguire, Jude Law and Christian Bale were all considered for the role of Will Turner, which was played by Orlando Bloom.

- Robert DeNiro was offered the role of Captain Jack Sparrow but declined.

- There have been a total of four very successful films in this series.

My Take: Johnny Depp does well in this role. I can see Bill Murray being even better.

Platoon (1986)

- Kyle MacLachlan was originally offered the role of Private Chris Taylor.

- Keanu Reeves turned down the role of Pvt. Chris Taylor.

- Oliver Stone directed and won the Academy Award for Best Director. He considered casting Johnny Depp as Pvt. Taylor but thought he was too young and unknown.

- Johnny Depp ended up playing the role of Lerner in the movie.

- Charlie Sheen was turned down for the role of Pvt. Chris Taylor at one point.

- Emilio Estevez, real life brother of Charlie Sheen, was then offered the part of Pvt. Taylor. Financial issues caused delays in filming. When the movie was ready to go Estevez was involved with other projects and unable to take the role.

- Charlie Sheen auditioned again and won the role of Private Chris Taylor.

- Kevin Costner was originally offered the role of Sergeant Barnes.

- Tom Berenger played Sgt. Barnes.

- Mickey Rourke was offered the role of Sgt. Barnes by Stone but said no.

- Nick Nolte was offered the role Sgt. Elias by Stone but he also declined.

- Willem Dafoe played Sgt. Elias.

- Jeff Bridges was considered for the role of Sgt. Elias.

- Kris Kristofferson was considered for a role.

- Oliver Stone wrote the first draft in 1971 sending it to singer Jim Morrison in hopes he would play the role of Pvt. Chris Taylor. Morrison had the script on him when he was found dead in Paris, France.

- Stone wanted James Woods to have a role in the movie but Woods turned the offer down.

- Val Kilmer auditioned for the film but was not offered a role.

- The film won the Academy Award for Best Picture.

My Take: This is one of those films where you can really see how external events can change the possibilities for the actors, which of course changes the film. I think Nick Nolte and Mickey Rourke would like this choice back.

Pulp Fiction (1994)

- Paul Calderon almost played the role of Jules Winnfield.

- Samuel. L. Jackson played Jules Winfield.

- Daniel Day Lewis wanted the role of Vincent Vega but Director Quentin Tarantino decided against it.

- John Travolta played Vincent Vega, which was his Hollywood comeback role.

- The role of Vincent Vega was written for Michael Madsen but his schedule would not allow him to take the role.

- Tarantino wanted Christopher Jones for the role of Zed.

- Peter Greene played Zed.

- Steve Buscemi refused the role of Jimmie Dimmick due to his schedule.

- Director Quentin Tarantino played Jimmie Dimmick

- Pam Grier auditioned for the role of Jody, Tarantino was not for her in that role.

- Rosanna Arquette played Jody.

- Sylvester Stallone and Mickey Rourke were both considered for the role of Butch, it is thought Stallone was actually offered the role which he declined.

- Bruce Willis played Butch.

- Bruce Willis wanted to play the role of Vincent Vega.

- Matt Dillon was in talks at one point to play Butch.

- Isabella Rossellini, Meg Ryan, Daryl Hannah, Joan Cusack and Michele Pfeiffer all interviewed for the role of Mia Wallace.

- Uma Thurman played Mia Wallace.

Raiders of the Lost Ark (1981)

- Harrison Ford played the lead role of Indiana Jones.

- Karen Allen played the lead role of Marion Ravenwood.

- Jeff Bridges and Steve Martin both turned down the lead role of Indiana Jones.

- Jack Nicholson and Nick Nolte were both considered for the lead role.

- Tom Selleck was the first choice of George Lucas to play Indiana, while Director Steven Spielberg wanted Harrison Ford. Tom Selleck wanted to take the role and film the movie. He was, at the time, set to start filming the first season of what would be his hit television show Magnum PI (1980). Despite the best efforts of Hollywood giants George Lucas and Steven Spielberg, CBS would not let Tom Selleck out of his contract to film the movie. Tom Selleck had to decide to break his contract and make the movie or honor his contract. Selleck decided to honor his contract with CBS and turned down the movie role. However there was a television writer's strike at that time which led to a delay in shooting Magnum PI. Raiders of the Lost Ark finished filming before Magnum PI ever started its own production. Tom Selleck would have been able to be Indiana Jones and start Magnum PI on time.

- Bill Murray was set to play the lead role but had to drop out due to his Saturday Night Live (1975) television schedule.

- Tim Matheson and Peter Coyote were considered for the lead.

- Amy Irving was considered for the role of Marion, in real life she is now the former Mrs. Stephen Spielberg.

- Debra Winger was also considered for the role of Marion.

- Danny Devito was wanted by Spielberg for the role of Sallah, which eventually went to Jonathan Rhys-Davies.

My Take: The best choice for the lead role was the first choice, Tom Selleck. He can play all the mannerisms that made Indiana Jones a great character and he can do it better then Harrison Ford. He proved it on Magnum PI (1980). It may be hard to think of a great film like this being even better but I believe it would have been. This is one of the casting calls I feel strongest about and one of the first reasons I had for this book. Tom Selleck's film career would have taken off and the Indiana movies would have continued to be a success. He is a great actor and more importantly a man of his word.

Rain Man (1988)

- Dustin Hoffman was supposed to play Charlie Babbitt.

- Tom Cruise played the role of Charlie Babbitt.

- Dustin Hoffman played Raymond Babbitt and won the Academy Award for Best Actor. Hoffman wanted Bill Murray to play Charlie Babbitt

- Barry Levinson directed and won the Academy Award for Best Director. He appeared in the movie as a psychiatrist.

- The movie was written with Dennis and Randy Quaid in mind as Charlie and Raymond.

- Jack Nicholson and Robert DeNiro both turned down the role of Raymond Babbitt.

- The film won the Academy Award for Best Picture.

My take: I think Bill Murray would have been better then Tom Cruise. Jack and DeNiro prove that even some of the best make mistakes when it comes to the casting call.

Rebecca (1940)

- The film won the Academy Award for Best Picture.

- Alfred Hitchcock directed.

- Margaret Sullavan, Vivien Leigh, Anne Baxter and Loretta Young all tested for the role of Mrs. de Winter.

- Anita Louise was also considered for the role.

- Joan Fontaine played Mrs. de Winter.

- Studio boss David O. Selznick wanted Olivia de Havilland or Carole Lombard for the female lead.

- Olivia de Havilland was committed to a Warner Bros. film and she was Joan Fontaine's real life sister, a fact the made her hesitant to take the part.

- O. Selznick wanted Ronald Coleman for the role of Maxim de Winter but Coleman declined.

- Laurence Olivier and William Powell were the backup choices to play Maxim.

- Laurence Olivier played Maxim de Winter.

Rebel Without a Cause (1955)

- Debbie Reynolds was suggested for the role of Judy, which was played by Natalie Wood.

- Margaret O'Brien and Jayne Mansfield tested for the role of Judy.

- James Dean played the lead role of Jim Stark.

Risky Business (1983)

- Timothy Hutton was the first choice to play Joel Goodsen.

- Nicholas Cage and Tom Hanks both auditioned for the role of Joel.

- Tom Cruise played Joel Goodsen.

- Kim Basinger was offered the role of Lana but turned it down.

- Diane Lane said Tom Cruise asked her to audition for the role of Lana.

- Rebecca De Mornay played Lana.

My take: I think Timothy Hutton and Nicholas Cage were the best choices for the role even though this is a movie Cruise is known for.

Robin Hood (2010)

- Christian Bale and Sam Riley were both considered for the lead role.

- Russell Crowe played the lead role of Robin Hood.

- Eileen Atkins replaced Natasha Richardson, wife of Liam Neeson, who died after a ski accident, in the role of Eleanor of Aquitaine.

- Rhys Ifans was considered for the role of King Richard.

- Danny Huston was cast as King Richard.

- Scarlett Johansson, Emily Blunt, Angelina Jolie and Natalie Portman were all considered for the role of Marian.

- Sienna Miller got the part of Marion but then dropped out.

- Annabelle Wallis, Rachel Weisz, Kate Winslet, Nicole Kidman, Naomi Watts and Charlize Theron were all then considered for the role of Marion.

- Kate Winslet, Cate Blanchett and Rachel Weisz were the top three choices, in that order, for the role of Marion.

- Kate Winslet declined the role, when Cate Blanchett accepted, they didn't approach Rachel Weisz.

My Take: Russell Crowe is always a good call. Rachel Weisz would have been my choice for Marion.

Rocky (1976)

- Sylvester Stallone played the lead character Rocky Balboa and also wrote the film. He was nearly broke at the time yet still turned down as much as five hundred thousand dollars for the movie rights, insisting that he play the lead role. Smart decision.

- United Artists Studios wanted Robert Redford, Ryan O'Neal, Burt Reynolds or James Caan to play the lead character Rocky Balboa.

- Carrie Snodgrass was offered the role of Adrian Balboa however she dropped out over a dispute about her salary.

- Lee Strasberg was offered the role of Mickey, but his salary demand was too high.

- Professional boxer Ken Norton was initially offered the role of Apollo Creed, but he was then thought to be too well known.

- Talia Shire, sister of famed movie director Francis Ford Coppola, played Adrian Balboa.

- Carl Weathers played Apollo Creed.

- Burgess Meredith played the role of Mickey.

- John G. Avildsen directed the film and won the Academy Award for Best Director.

- The film won the Academy Award for Best Picture.

My Take: Clearly I am a fan of Burt Reynolds. However everyone knows that nobody could have played this role except for Sylvester Stallone. He was nominated for an Academy Award for Best Actor and Best Screenplay. Only two other individuals were ever nominated in those categories in the same year. Charlie Chaplin (1940) and Orson Welles (1941). That is pretty good company and answers those who like to denigrate his talent.

Roman Holiday (1953)

- The first choices for the role of Princess Ann: Jean Simmons, Suzanne Cloutier and Elizabeth Taylor.

- Audrey Hepburn played Princess Ann and won the Academy Award for Best Actress.

- The male lead role of Joe Bradley was written with Cary Grant in mind, he declined the role thinking he was too old.

- Gregory Peck played Joe Bradley.

Rush Hour (1998)

- Martin Lawrence was the original choice to play the role of James Carter.

- Dave Chapelle was also considered for James Carter.

- Eddie Murphy was offered the role of James Carter, he declined due his schedule. He chose to instead film the movie Holy Man (1998).

- Chris Tucker played Detective James Carter.

- Jackie Chan played Detective Inspector Lee.

My Take: I think Eddie Murphy regrets that decision. Martin Lawrence would have been interesting. Chris Tucker did play the role at a top level.

Saving Private Ryan (1998)

- Mel Gibson and Harrison Ford were both considered for the role of Captain John Miller.
- Tom Hanks played Captain John H. Miller.
- Michael Madsen was offered the role of Sergeant Mike Horvath, he turned the role down but did suggest his friend Tom Sizemore.
- Tom Sizemore played Sergeant Mike Horvath.
- Edward Norton turned down the role of Private James Francis Ryan.
- Matt Damon played Private James Francis Ryan.
- Vin Diesel played Private Adrian Caparzo a role that was written for him.

- Steven Spielberg directed and won the Academy Award for Best Director.

Scareface (1983)

- Robert DeNiro was offered the lead role of Tony Montana but turned it down.

- Al Pacino played Tony Montana.

- John Travolta was once considered for the role of Manny Ribera.

- Steven Bauer played Manny Ribera.

- Brooke Shields was offered the lead role of Elvira Hancock but it is said her mother made her decline the part.

- Kim Basinger, Jodie Foster, Melanie Griffith, Kathleen Turner, Jennifer Jason Leigh, and Rosanna Arquette all turned down the role of Elvira.

- Carrie Fisher, Geena Davis, Kelly McGillis and Sharon Stone auditioned for the role of Elvira.

- Kay Lenz and Kristy McNichol were rumored to have wanted the role of Elvira but were turned down by the director, Brian De Palma.

- Michelle Pfeiffer played Elvira Hancock.

Sea of Love (1989)

- The lead role of Detective Frank Keller was written for Dustin Hoffman. However he wanted too many rewrites and was then replaced.

- Al Pacino played Detective Frank Keller, which was a comeback for him.

My Take: Dustin Hoffman saying no was a huge break for Pacino, who was in a major slump. He has been getting good roles ever since. Hard to imagine but even Academy Award winners need some help with their career.

Sergeant York (1941)

- Henry Fonda, James Stewart and Ronald Reagan were all considered for the lead role of Alvin C. York.

- Gary Cooper played Alvin C. York and won the Academy Award for Best Actor.

- Jane Russell was considered for the role of Gracie Williams.

- Joan Leslie played Gracie Williams.

- Helen Wood, Linda Hayes and Susan Peters all tested for the role of Gracie.

- Pat O'Brien and Ronald Reagan actually tested for Sergeant York.

- Mary Nash tested for Mother York which was played by Margaret Wycherly.

The Seven Year Itch (1955)

- Director Billy Wilder wanted to cast Walter Matthau as the lead character Richard Sherman but 20th Century Fox Studio decided against that.

- Tom Ewell played Richard Sherman, a role he had already played in the Broadway version of this story.

- Vanessa Brown played The Girl on Broadway but was replaced when the film went from Paramount Studios to 20th Century Fox.

- Marilyn Monroe played The Girl in the film.

- Gary Cooper was considered for the role of Richard Sherman.

- George Cukor was the original choice to direct.

- The film premiered on June 1, 1955 which just happened to be the 29th birthday of Marilyn Monroe.

My Take: Tom Ewell was hilarious. This is one of Marilyn Monroe's two best films hands down and in my opinion her best performance in any film. If you have not seen this film you are missing a great comedy.

The Shining (1980)

- Harrison Ford, Robin Williams and Robert DeNiro were all considered by Director Stanley Kubrick for the role of Jack Torrence.

- Stephen King, the author of The Shining, wanted Jon Voight or Michael Moriarty to play Jack Torrence, not Jack Nicholson.

- Jack Nicholson did play the role of Jack Torrence.

- Harry Dean Stanton was the original choice for Lloyd the Bartender but his schedule did not allow it, the role was then played by Joe Turkel.

The Shootist (1976)

- John Wayne played J.B. Books. It was his last film.

- George C. Scott was offered the role of Books, but it was given to John Wayne after he showed interest and because he was the first choice all along.

- Maureen O'Hara was considered for the role Bond Rogers but Director Don Siegel thought she wasn't the right fit. She had starred in many films with John Wayne.

- John Wayne selected Lauren Bacall for the role of Bond Rogers, which she played.

- John Wayne requested James Stewart for the movie, he played Dr. E.W.Hostetler.

My Take: Maureen O'Hara always had great chemistry with John Wayne at any age. I think she would have been the best choice in this film. Ron Howard had one of his early adult roles in this film. This is a solid movie.

The Silence of the Lambs (1991)

- Director Jonathan Demme wanted Michelle Pfeiffer to play Clarice Starling. She turned the role down feeling the movie was to violent. He won the Academy Award for Best Director.

- Meg Ryan and Melanie Griffith both turned down the role of Clarice because the subject matter was disturbing.

- Jodie Foster played Clarice Starling and won the Academy Award for Best Actress.

- John Hurt, Christopher Lloyd, Patrick Stewart, Louis Gossett Jr., Jack Nicholson, Robert Duvall and Robert DeNiro were all considered for the role of Dr. Hannibal Lecter.

- Jeremy Irons turned down the role of Lecter.

- Sean Connery was the first choice of Director Jonathan Demme to play Lecter. He declined the role.

- Anthony Hopkins played Dr. Hannibal Lecter and won the Academy Award for Best Actor.

- Kenneth Branagh, Michael Keaton and Mickey Rourke were considered for the role of Jack Crawford.

- Scott Glenn played Jack Crawford.

- The film won the Academy Award for Best Picture.

- One of three films to win all five major Academy Awards.

Singin' in the Rain (1952)

- Judy Garland, June Allyson, Ann Miller, Jane Powell and Leslie Caron were all considered for the role of Kathy Selden.

- Debbie Reynolds, wife of Eddie Fischer and mother of Carrie Fischer, played the role of Kathy Selden.

- Howard Keel was the original choice for Don Lockwood.

- Gene Kelly played the role of Don Lockwood.

- Carol Haney was recommended by Gene Kelly for the role of Kathy Selden.

- Judy Holliday was the first choice for the role of Lina Lamont.

- The role of Lina was played by Jean Hagen.

- The role of Cosmo Brown was written for Oscar Levant.

- Donald O'Connor played the role of Cosmo Brown.

Sleepless in Seattle (1993)

- The role of Annie Reed was originally offered to Julia Roberts, she turned it down. Another role for Charisma Carpenter.

- Kim Basinger was offered the role of Annie early on. She turned it down due to her doubt in the premise of the film.

- Jodie Foster, Michelle Pfeiffer and Jennifer Jason Leigh turned down the role of Annie, eventually played by Meg Ryan

Some Like it Hot (1959)

- Jack Lemmon played the lead role of Jerry/Daphne.

- Tony Curtis played the lead role of Joe/Josephine/Shell Oil Junior.

- Marilyn Monroe played the female lead role of Sugar Kane Kowalczyk.

- Director Billy Wilder wanted Frank Sinatra for the role of Jerry/ Daphne.

- Director Billy Wilder also wanted Mitzi Gaynor for the role of Sugar until learning that Marilyn Monroe was available.

- Jerry Lewis was offered the role of Jerry/ Daphne, but he turned it down.

- Bob Hope was considered for the role of Joe/Josephine.

- Danny Kaye was considered for the role of Jerry/Daphne.

My Take: One of the funniest films ever. This is the other of Marilyn Monroe's two best movies and roles.

The Sound of Music (1965)

- Sean Connery, Richard Burton and Yul Brynner were all considered for the role of Captain Von Trapp.

- Christopher Plummer played the role of Captain Von Trapp.

- Paramount Studios, as film rights owners, wanted Audrey Hepburn for the role of Maria however she said no.

- Julie Andrews played Maria.

- Kurt Russell, Richard Dreyfuss, Patty Duke, Alan, Jay, Merrill and Wayne Osmond all auditioned for the children's roles.

- Doris Day was offered the role of Maria, she turned it down.

- Leslie Ann Warren and Mia Farrow auditioned for the role of Liesl Von Trapp.

- Jeanette MacDonald was considered for the role of Mother Abbess, which was played by Peggy Wood.

- Robert Wise directed and won the Academy Award for Best Director.
- The film won the Academy Award for Best Picture.

My Take: This is one of the most financially successful films ever made. It is a good quality family film.

The Specialist (1994)

- The film was offered to Steven Seagal, a project where he would direct and star as Ray Quick but he wanted too much money.
- Sylvester Stallone was then offered the project.
- The studio said Stallone had to commit right away or they would replace him with Warren Beatty.
- Sylvester Stallone played Ray Quick.
- Sharon Stone played May Munro, aka Adrian Hastings.

My Take: Stallone and Stone, come on. Well maybe just Stallone. I could see Seagal in this role but not Warren Beatty. I would have given the female lead to Vanity over Stone.

Speed (1994)

- The role of Jack Traven, played by Keanu Reeves, was written with Jeff Bridges in mind.

- Harold "Harry" Temple, played by Jeff Daniels was intended to be played by Ed Harris.

- George Clooney, Johnny Depp, Stephen Baldwin, William Baldwin, Bruce Willis, Arnold Schwarzenegger, Michael Keaton and Tom Cruise were all considered for the role of Jack Traven.

- John McTiernan, Renny Harlin and Quentin Tarantino declined the opportunity to direct Speed.

- Jan de Bont directed and insisted on Sandra Bullock for the role of Annie Porter, against studio wishes.

- Glenn Close, Barbara Hershey, Jessica Lange, Sigourney Weaver, Jane Seymour, Kay Lenz, Kim Basinger, Halle Berry, Debra Winger, Kathleen Turner, Geena Davis, Carrie Fisher, Melanie Griffith, Michelle Pfeiffer, Emma Thompson, Rosanna Arquette, Meg Tilly, Daryl Hannah, Meg Ryan,

Jennifer Jason Leigh, Ally Sheedy, Demi Moore, Jodie Foster, Tatum O'Neal, Bridget Fonda, Marisa Tomei, Diane Lane, Sarah Jessica Parker, Brooke Shields, Julia Roberts, Winona Ryder, Cameron Diaz and Alyssa Milano all turned down the role of Annie Porter.

My Take: This was a career making movie for both Keanu and Bullock. Jeff Bridges would have been good but Keanu pulled it off. I think Marisa Tomei, Bridget Fonda, Kay Lenz or Brooke Shields would have done well. I also think they wish they would have taken the role. Charisma Carpenter would have been great.

Spiderman (2002)

- Nicolas Cage, John Malkovich and Robert DeNiro were offered the role of Norman Osborn/Green Goblin.

- Willem Dafoe played Norman Osborn/Green Goblin.

- Tobey Maguire played Peter Parker/Spiderman

- James Franco wanted the role of Peter Parker however he played Harry Osborne.

- Leonardo DiCaprio was considered for the role of Peter Parker.

- Directors Jan de Bont, Tony Scott and James Cameron among others, were considered as director.

- Sam Raimi directed the film.

- Kirsten Dunst played Mary Jane Watson.

- Alicia Witt was considered for the role of Mary Jane Watson.

- Mena Suvari and Elisha Cuthbert auditioned for Mary Jane Watson.

- Scott Speedman tested for Peter Parker.

- Marion Ross (of televisions Happy Days, 1974) was considered for the role of "Aunt" May Parker.

- Rosemary Harris played May Parker.

- Edward Norton was offered the role of Harry Osborn/Green Goblin, but was already scheduled to film Red Dragon (2002).

- In the previous decade all of the following actresses were considered for Mary Jane Watson: Jennifer Aniston, Tatum O'Neal, Phoebe Cates, Jodie Foster, Ally Sheedy, Brooke Shields, Molly Ringwald, Nicole Kidman, Bridget Fonda, Lori

Loughlin, and Diane Lane. All were considered too old when the film actually began trying to fill the role.

My Take: The movie carried itself. I think Nadia Bjorlin would have made a fantastic Mary Jane.

Stagecoach (1939)

- Gary Cooper was wanted for the role of Ringo Kid.

- Bruce Cabot tested for the role of Ringo.

- Director John Ford gave the role to his first choice, John Wayne.

- John Ford wanted Ward Bond for the role of Buck the stage driver, he couldn't drive so the role went to Andy Devine.

- David O. Selznick, the studio head, wanted Marlene Dietrich for the role of Dallas.

- Claire Trevor played Dallas.

- Thomas Mitchell played Doc Boone and won the Academy Award for Best Supporting Actor.

My Take: John Wayne in a western can't miss and this one does not.

Star Wars (1977)

- Actors considered for the role of Han Solo: Kurt Russell, Nick Nolte, Christopher Walken, Jack Nicholson, Al Pacino, Chevy Chase, Steve Martin, Bill Murray and Perry King.

- Actresses who auditioned for the role of Princess Leia: Kay Lenz, Farrah Fawcett, Glenn Close, Barbara Hershey, Bernadette Peters, Bonnie Bedelia, Dianne Wiest, Margot Kidder, Jessica Lange, Meryl Streep, Sigourney Weaver, Cybill Shepard, Christine Lahti, Jane Seymour, Anjelica Huston, Catherine Hicks, Christine Baranski, Kim Basinger, Kathleen Turner, Debra Winger, Cindy Williams and Geena Davis.

- Melanie Griffith was once offered the role of Princess Leia. The role eventually went to Carrie Fischer, daughter of Eddie Fischer and Debbie Reynolds.

- Burt Reynolds, Al Pacino, Jack Nicholson, Robert DeNiro and James Caan all turned down the role of Han Solo.

- Mel Blanc, the voice of Warner Brother's cartoons, auditioned for the voice of C3PO, which went to Anthony Daniels.

- George Lucas wanted Orson Welles for the voice of Darth Vader however he then thought his voice was too recognized. The voice role went to James Earl Jones.

- George Lucas directed.

My Take: You guessed it, I think Burt Reynolds would have been the best choice for Han Solo. I think all those actors wish they had accepted the role though. Kay Lenz would have made a great Princess Leia because she was not overexposed and is a good actress. The success of this series is well known with three more movies in the works bringing the end total to nine.

Star Trek (2009)

- Director J.J. Abrams said the only choices for Nero were Russell Crowe and Eric Bana.

- Eric Bana played the role of Nero.

- Mike Vogel and Chris Pine were the final two choices to play Captain James T. Kirk.

- Chris Pine played Captain Kirk. After getting the role he sent a letter to William Shatner (Captain Kirk in the television show Star Trek, 1966) and received a reply where Shatner gave his approval to Pine.

- Matt Damon contacted Director J.J. Abrams when he heard he was being considered for the role of Kirk. Abrams replied with a "no", he thought Damon was too old.

- Josh Lucas was considered for the role of Christopher Pike.

- Bruce Greenwood played the role of Christopher Pike.

- Sydney Tamiia Poitier auditioned for the role of Uhura.

- Zoe Salanda played Uhura.

- Keri Russell was considered for a role in the film.

Stripes (1981)

- Originally this film was to be a project for Cheech and Chong. Their agent asked for too much future money so that plan was scrapped.

- Dennis Quaid has an unseen role in the graduation parade scene.

- Ivan Reitman said Bill Murray insisted on Harold Ramis being given the role of Russell Ziskey, a role Ramis did play. Murray wanted Ramis to help him rewrite his dialogue and to improvise. Bill Murray and Harold Ramis were also close friends in real life.

- Kim Basinger was offered the part of M.P. Stella Hanson according to Ivan Reitman. Her agent then asked for too much money.

- P.J. Soles played the role of M.P. Stella Hanson.

- Timothy Busfield made his film debut.

- Ivan Reitman directed the film.

My Take: I can't think of this film without Bill Murray. Kim Basinger should have overruled her agent.

Superman Returns (2005)

- Actresses considered for the role of Lois Lane: Elisha Cuthbert, Claire Danes and Keri Russell.

- Kate Bosworth played the role of Lois Lane.

- Actors considered for the role of Clark Kent/Superman: Josh Hartnett, Paul Walker, Matthew Bomer, Brendan Fraser, Ashton Kutcher, David Boreanaz, Henry Cavill, Jerry O'Connell and Hayden Christenson.

- The director at the time Brett Ratner, wanted his personal choice which was Henry Cavill.

- Brandon Routh played Clark Kent/Superman.

- When Director Tim Burton was involved, he wanted Ralph Fiennes or David Duchovny as Superman.

- While Brett Ratner was still involved, Anthony Hopkins was set to play Jor-El of Krypton. Hopkins left the project when Ratner did.

- Johnny Depp was considered for the role of Lex Luthor.

- Kevin Spacey played the role of Lex Luthor.

- Scarlett Johansson was considered for the role of Lois Lane.

- Shia LaBeouf, Topher Grace, and Shawn Ashmore were all considered for the role of Jimmy Olsen.

- Sam Huntington played Jimmy Olsen.

- Director Bryan Singer wanted Jude Law as General Zod, but he said no so the role was cut.

- Jim Caviezel wanted to play Superman but Singer said no because he was too famous after his starring role as Jesus in The Passion of The Christ 2004.

- Keira Knightley and Mischa Barton were considered for the role of Lois Lane.

- Kate Bosworth played Lois Lane.

- Hugh Laurie was set to play Perry White but had to drop out due to the filming of his television series, House (2004).

- Frank Langella played the role of Perry White.

- Billy Zane was considered for the role of Lex Luthor.

- Filmmaker Jon Peters wanted Beyonce Knowles, Jennifer Lopez or Catherine Zeta-Jones for the role of Lois Lane.

- Will Smith was said to have turned down the lead role.

My Take: Jim Caviezel is easily the best choice here for Superman. He would have been great. As I said earlier in Man of Steel (2013), I would have cast real life reporter Andrea Tantaros as Lois Lane in this film as well. She has the smarts and beauty the character calls for and would have brought fresh energy into this series restart. With these two choices we may have had two more Superman films already.

Tequila Sunrise (1988)

- Harrison Ford was interested at one point before dropping out.

- The film at one time was supposed to star real life friends Nick Nolte and Jeff Bridges. Nolte was going to play Detective Nicholas Frescia and Bridges would have played Dale McKussic.

- Mel Gibson played Dale 'Mac' McKussic.

- Kurt Russell played Detective Nicholas 'Nick' Frescia.

The Terminator (1984)

- Arnold Schwarzenegger played The Terminator.

- Mel Gibson turned down the role of The Terminator.

- Jurgen Prochnow and O.J. Simpson were considered for the role of The Terminator.

- Lance Henrikson was strongly considered for the role of The Terminator.

- Edward James Olmos and Lou Gossett Jr. were both considered for the role of Lt. Traxler.

- Director James Cameron originally wanted Arnold to play Kyle Reese.

- Kyle Reese was played by Michael Biehn.

- Cameron also wanted Bridget Fonda for the role of Sarah Connor. Fonda was at one point replaced by Tatum O'Neal. When the role of Sarah Connor was aged, Cameron wanted Kate Capshaw or Kathleen Turner to play Sarah, both said no to the role due to their schedules.

- Deborah Winger auditioned and won the role but then dropped out.

- Daryl Hannah turned down the role of Sarah Connor due to her schedule.

- Linda Hamilton played Sarah Connor in the movie.

- Sylvester Stallone was offered the lead role and turned it down, he could have done well in the role as he was at one of his box office peaks.

- Other Actresses considered for the role of Sarah Connor: Glenn Close, Sigourney Weaver, Cybill Shepherd, Jane Seymour, Lori Loughlin, Kim Basinger, Jodie Foster, Melanie Griffith, Christy Brinkley, Jamie Lee Curtis, Ally Sheedy, Jessica Lange,

Sissy Spacek, Kay Lenz, Liza Minelli (daughter of Judy Garland), Mia Farrow, Barbara Hershey, Miranda Richardson, Rosanna Arquette, Meg Ryan, Heather Locklear, Madonna, Amy Irving, and Teri Garr.

- Randy Quaid, Kevin Kline and Michael Douglas were all considered for the lead role.

- Tom Selleck was offered the lead role, he had to decline due to his schedule.

- Sharon Stone and Kellie McGillis auditioned for Sarah Connor.

- Geena Davis, Michele Pfeiffer, Diane Lane and Carrie Fisher were also considered for the role of Sarah.

- At one point Glenn Close was chosen and dropped out due to her schedule.

My Take: Tom Selleck misses out again due to his schedule. He is a legit six feet four inches tall and would have made an intimidating terminator. This movie seemed to grow in reputation years after its release.

Titanic (1997)

- James Cameron directed and won the Academy Award for Best Director.

- The Studio wanted Matthew McConoughey for the lead role of Jack Dawson, but James Cameron insisted on Leonardo DiCaprio, who did get the part.

- Jack Davenport was considered for the part of Caledon "Cal" Hockley but was thought to be too young.

- Billy Zane played Caledon "Cal" Hockley.

- Michael Caine may have refused a role in the film.

- Macaulay Culkin was considered for the role of Jack Dawson.

- Reba McEntire was offered and accepted the role of Molly Brown, but dropped out due to a schedule conflict.

- Kathy Bates played the role of Molly.

- Dolores O'Riordan (Lead singer for the Cranberries rock band) was offered the opportunity to act and compose but said no because she was about to give birth.

- Michael Biehn was almost cast as Cal.

- Rob Lowe and Pierce Brosnan were also considered for the role of Cal.

- Christian Bale auditioned for the role of Jack Dawson.

- Gwyneth Paltrow was up for the role of Rose Dewitt Baker.

- Kate Winslet won the role of Rose Dewitt Baker.

- Fay Wray and Ann Rutherford were both offered the role of "older" Rose but said no.

- Gloria Stuart played the role of "older" Rose.

- Robert DeNiro was offered the role of Captain Edward James Smith but declined.

- Bernard Hill played the role of Captain Smith.

- Nicole Kidman was considered for the role of Rose.

- Madonna auditioned for the role of Rose.

- The film won the Academy Award for Best Picture.

- The film won eleven Academy Awards which tied the motion picture Ben- Hur (1959) for the most all time.

My Take: Financially successful and awards were plentiful. I'm not quite sure why it reached the level it did in either area.

To Kill a Mockingbird (1962)

- James Stewart was considered for the lead role of Atticus Finch.

- Gregory Peck played Atticus Finch and won the Academy Award for Best Actor.

Top Gun (1986)

- Nicholas Cage, John Cusack, Sean Penn, Matthew Broderick, Michael J. Fox and Emilio Estevez all turned down the role of Maverick.

- Jim Carrey, Charlie Sheen, Rob Lowe, Eric Stoltz, John Travolta, Scott Baio, and Robert Downey Jr. were considered for the role of Maverick.

- Maverick was played by Tom Cruise.

- Charlie was played by Kelley McGillis.

- This film was not only the major box office breakthrough for Tom Cruise but is also one of the highest grossing military themed films of all time.

- Tatum O'Neal, Holly Hunter, Michelle Pfeiffer, Jennifer Grey, Jamie Lee Curtis, Ally Sheedy, Geena Davis, Jodie Foster, Daryl Hannah, Diane Lane, Sarah Jessica Parker, Linda Hamilton and Brooke Shields all turned down the role of Charlie.

- Carrie Fisher, Sharon Stone, Debra Winger, Olivia Newton John and Madonna were considered for the role of Charlie.

- Lou Gossett Jr. was considered for the role of Viper.

- Tom Skerritt played Viper.

- REO Speedwagon and Toto were considered to perform the theme song.

- Kenny Loggins recorded the hit theme song, Danger Zone.

- Tony Scott, brother of director Ridley Scott, was the director.

My Take: I think all the actors and actresses listed regret turning the lead roles down.

Total Recall (1990)

- Jeff Bridges was considered for the lead role of Douglas Quaid/Hauser.

- Matthew Broderick and Richard Dreyfuss were considered for the role of Douglas Quaid/Hauser.

- Arnold Schwarzenegger played Douglas Quaid/Hauser.

- Robert Davi and Kurtwood Smith turned down the role of Richter.

- Michael Ironside played Richter.

- Sharon Stone played Lori. Her role as a woman who changed from shy to vixen seemingly at will, was the basis for a character that Paul Verhoeven would eventually make a movie around starring Stone, Basic Instinct (1992).

- Paul Verhoeven directed the film.

My Take: Given the time the movie was made I think the only other actors who could have played this role successfully were Stallone, Bruce Willis or Mel Gibson.

Trading Places (1983)

- Ray Milland was the first choice to play Mortimer Duke, which was played by Don Ameche.

- This film was part of the run that made Eddie Murphy a box office draw.

- The original plans called for the film to have Gene Wilder play Louis Winthorpe III and Richard Pryor play Billy Ray Valentine. The pair had starred together twice already in the movies Silver Streak (1976) and Stir Crazy (1980).

- Dan Aykroyd played Louis Winthorpe III.

- Eddie Murphy played Billy Ray Valentine. He wanted to play opposite an actor other then Gene Wilder to avoid comparisons between himself and Richard Pryor.

- The role of Clarence Beeks was offered to G. Gordon Liddy but he said no, Paul Gleason played the role.

- John Gielgud was offered the role of Coleman the butler which was played by Denholm Elliot.

My Take: Eddie Murphy was excellent and the best choice for his role. Gene Wilder would have been as good as Aykroyd in my opinion.

True Grit (1969)

- John Wayne played the lead role of Marshal Rueben J. "Rooster" Cogburn.

- John Wayne won the Academy Award for Best Actor.

- John Wayne wanted the role of Mattie Ross to go to his daughter Aissa Wayne however director Henry Hathaway would not give her the role.

- Mia Farrow was approached for the role of Mattie Ross but decided against it.

- Elvis Presley was considered for the role of La Boeuf but his manager "Colonel" Tom Parker messed the negotiations up. What a surprise.

- Singer Glen Campbell played the role instead of Elvis.

- Tuesday Weld turned down the role of Mattie.

- Sally Field and Sondra Locke were both up for the role of Mattie.

My Take: Two items stand out. Even if John Wayne had not won the Academy Award for Best Actor, which he did, no one else past or present could have played this role at his level. Elvis Presley absolutely would have made any film better.

The Untouchables (1987)

- Bob Hoskins was approached about the role of Al Capone.
- Robert DeNiro played Al Capone.
- Michael Douglas, Don Johnson, Mel Gibson, and Harrison Ford all said no to playing the role of Eliot Ness.
- Kevin Costner played FBI agent Eliot Ness.
- Jack Nicholson was offered the role of Eliot Ness and turned it down.
- William Hurt was considered for Eliot Ness but had to decline due to his schedule.

- Director Brian DePalma discussed the role of Eliot Ness with Nick Nolte, Tom Berenger, and Jeff Bridges.

- Gene Hackman was under consideration for the role of Jim Malone.

- Sean Connery played Jim Malone and won the Academy Award for Best Supporting Actor.

The Usual Suspects (1995)

- Robert DeNiro and Christopher Walken both turned down the role of U.S. Customs agent Dave Kujan.

- Chazz Palminteri played Dave Kujan..

- Michael Biehn turned down the role of Michael McManus.

- Stephen Baldwin played Michael McManus.

- Al Pacino read for the role of Dave Kujan but he had to say no due to schedule conflicts.

- Kevin Spacey played Roger "Verbal" Kint and won the Academy Award for Best Supporting Actor.

When Harry Met Sally (1989)

- Albert Brooks turned down the role of Harry Burns.

- Billy Crystal played Harry Burns.

- Molly Ringwald was offered the role of Sally Albright but had to decline due to her schedule.

- Meg Ryan played Sally Albright.

- Rob Reiner (Michael "Meathead" Stivic from televisions All in the Family, 1971) directed this film.

The Wizard of Oz (1939)

- W.C. Fields was wanted to play the Wizard however the money required to hire him was too much.

- Ray Bolger was originally set to play the Tin Woodsman.

- Buddy Ebsen (of televisions Beverly Hillbillies, 1962) was originally set to play the Scarecrow.

- Bolger and Ebsen switched roles, then Ebsen dropped out and Jack Haley took over as the Tin Woodsman.

- Judy Garland was always first choice to play Dorothy, Shirley Temple and Deanna Durbin were considered as back up options.

My Take: Judy Garland owns this role and she can really sing.

The Woman in Red (1984)

- Melanie Griffith turned down the role of Charlotte to film Body Double (1984).

- Kelly Le Brock played Charlotte.

- Gene Wilder, who played the male lead character Teddy Pierce, also directed.

My Summary:

I learned a few things writing this. If an actor or actress I like is in a film, I will see it even if I know little about the film. There are some movies that should never be remade. Usually that is due to the outstanding performances by the actors and/or actresses in the films. Hollywood, with some films, leave great enough alone.

You were probably wondering: In addition to the two films profiled in this book, **It Happened One Night (1934)** and **Silence of the Lambs (1991),** the third film to win all five main Academy Awards (Best Picture, Director, Actor, Actress and Screenplay) is **One Flew Over the Cuckoo's Nest (1975).** Unfortunately, another missed opportunity for Burt Reynolds.

The Lord of the Rings: The Return of the King (2003) won eleven Academy Awards joining **Ben-Hur (1959)** and **Titanic (1997)** for the most all time.

Sources:

- Internet Movie Data Base.com

- Sports Illustrated, August 2, 2010, Chris Nashawaty.

- Turner Classic Movie Channel

- Panorama Magazine (Exorcist) via IMDB.com

- Variety Magazine (Exorcist) via IMDB.com

The Bourne Identity (2002)	20
The Breakfast Club (1985)	21
The Bridge Over the River Kwai (1957)	22
Broken Arrow (1996)	24
Butch Cassidy & The Sundance Kid (1969)	24
Caddy Shack (1980)	25
Casablanca (1942)	27
Casino Royale (2006)	28
Charlie & the Chocolate Factory (2005)	29
Charlie's Angels (2000)	30
Cinderella Man (2005)	31
Code of Silence (1985)	32
Copland (1997)	32
Death Wish (1974)	33
Deliverance (1972)	34
Demolition Man (1993)	35
Die Hard (1988)	35
Dirty Harry (1971)	37
The Doors (1991)	39

Laura (1944)	82
Lawrence of Arabia (1962)	83
Live & Let Die (1973)	84
Live Free or Die Hard (2007)	85
The Living Daylights (1987)	86
The Lord of the Rings (2001)	88
The Maltese Falcon (1941)	90
Man of Steel (2013)	90
Manhunter (1986)	93
The Matrix (1999)	94
Maverick (1994)	95
Meet the Parents (2000)	96
Men In Black (1997)	96
Miami Vice (2006)	97
Mr. & Mrs. Smith (2005)	98
North By Northwest (1959)	99
The Omen (1976)	100
On The Waterfront (1954)	100
The Pink Panther (1964)	102

Pirates of the Caribbean (2003)	103
Platoon (1986)	104
Pulp Fiction (1994)	106
Raiders of the Lost Ark (1981)	107
Rain Man (1988)	109
Rebecca (1940)	110
Rebel Without A Cause (1955)	111
Risky Business (1983)	112
Robin Hood (2010)	113
Rocky (1976)	114
Roman Holiday (1953)	116
Rush Hour (1998)	116
Saving Private Ryan (1998)	117
Scarface (1983)	118
Sea of Love (1989)	119
Sergeant York (1941)	120
The Seven Year Itch (1955)	120
The Shining (1980)	122
The Shootist (1976)	122

Made in the USA
Monee, IL
13 March 2021